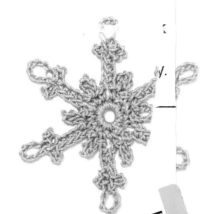

100 Snowflakes to Crochet

100 Snowflakes to Crochet

Caitlin Sainio

Search Press

A QUARTO BOOK

Published in 2012 by Search Press Ltd
Wellwood
North Farm Road
Tunbridge Wells
Kent TN2 3DR

ISBN: 978-1-84448-805-6

Conceived, designed and produced by
Quarto Publishing plc
The Old Brewery
6 Blundell Street
London N7 9BH

QUAR: HCKS

Senior Editor: Ruth Patrick
Art Editor and Designer: Jackie Palmer
Pattern Checker: Lucia Calza
Illustrator: Coral Mula, Kuo Kang Chen
Photography (showcase and technical section): Simon Pask
Photography (projects): Nicki Dowey
Proofreader: Sally MacEachern
Indexer: Helen Snaith
Art Director: Caroline Guest
Creative Director: Moira Clinch
Publisher: Paul Carslake

Color separation by PICA Digital Pte Ltd, Singapore
Printed by 1010 Printing International Ltd, China

CONTENTS

Foreword   6
About this book   6

1 THE BASICS   8
    Tools and materials   10
    Patterns and abbreviations   12
    Crochet refresher course   14

2 SNOWFLAKE SHOWCASE   20

3 SNOWFLAKE PATTERNS   42
    Beginner patterns   44
    Intermediate patterns   60
    Advanced patterns   86

4 PROJECTS   110
    Project 1: Toasty hat and mittens   112
    Project 2: Gift tags and cards   114
    Project 3: Magical mobile   116
    Project 4: Accent pillows   118
    Project 5: Hanging snowflakes   120
    Project 6: Framed snowflake art   122
    Project 7: Blizzard scarf   124

Index   126
Acknowledgements   128

FOREWORD

I was first introduced to crochet by elementary school classmates, who taught me a few stitches and left me so delighted that I appropriated one of my mother's crochet books to teach myself more. A few years later, I discovered thread crochet and fell completely in love: the process of turning smooth thread into delicate lace was, and still is, as magical to me as spinning straw into gold.

Snowflakes are among my favourite subjects to crochet, partly because real snowflakes are so lovely, and partly because crochet is a wonderful medium for creating snowflake shapes. The stitches build on one another just as tiny ice crystals do, and the finished pieces are as beautiful, graceful and varied as their frosty counterparts. This collection is designed to capture that beauty, grace and variety, and my hope is that it will provide both novice and experienced crocheters with many hours of inspiration and enjoyment.

Caitlin Sainio

ABOUT THIS BOOK

This book presents an enchanting selection of 100 snowflake patterns for you to crochet, as well as a selection of stunning and inspirational project ideas. Each of these delicate creations can be used to embellish garments, gifts, accessories, homewares and much more.

SECTION 1: THE BASICS
(PAGES 8–19)

The book begins with basic crochet information about equipment, symbols, abbreviations and terminology, as well as some notes on how to work the key stitches featured in the book. If you are new to crochet or just need a refresher, you will find all of the know-how you need to get started.

SECTION 2: SNOWFLAKE SHOWCASE
(PAGES 20–41)

The Showcase displays the 100 beautiful designs that feature in this book. Flick through this colourful visual guide, select your design and then turn to the relevant page of instructions to create your chosen piece.

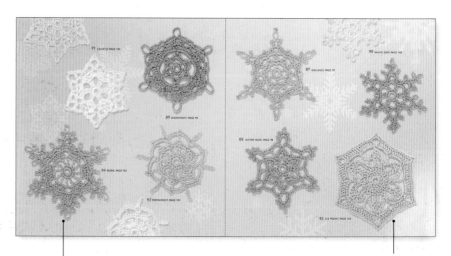

Each design is shown at actual size and in proportion to the others on the page, which gives an idea of size and scale.

Each item is labelled with its name and number that corresponds to the relevant instructions in the Snowflake patterns chapter (pages 42–109).

SECTION 3: SNOWFLAKE PATTERNS
(PAGES 42–109)

In this chapter you'll find instructions on how to create every design featured in the Showcase. The snowflake designs each feature a chart, finished photograph, and written instructions. This is so that you can use either method or, better still, combine both. All the snowflakes have been designed for size 10 thread and a 1.90mm (size 5) hook, and the patterns are organized by degree of difficulty – beginner, intermediate or advanced.

Full instructions are provided for each snowflake design.

The difficulty level of the patterns is indicated at the edge of each page: beginner, intermediate or advanced.

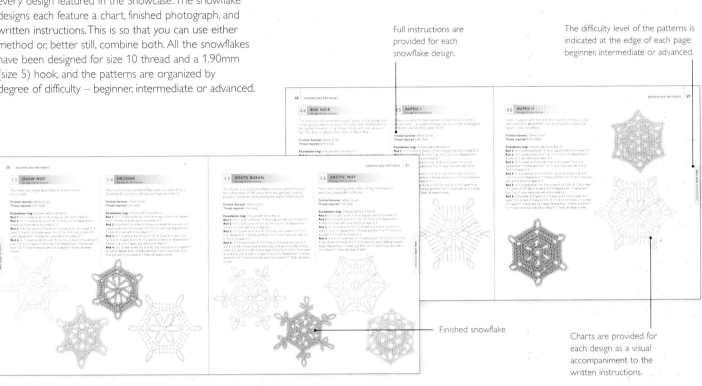

Finished snowflake

Charts are provided for each design as a visual accompaniment to the written instructions.

SECTION 4: PROJECTS
(PAGES 110–125)

The beauty of these snowflake designs is that they can all be used to embellish a number of items, from garments and gifts to home accessories. This chapter presents a selection of ideas to inspire and encourage you to use the featured designs in a variety of ways.

A close-up photograph of each project shows in detail how the item has been made and put together.

Each project is illustrated with a photograph of the finished item.

THE BASICS

In this chapter, you will find detailed information on tools, materials and patterns, as well as all of the crochet and finishing techniques that you'll need to make the snowflakes in the Snowflake patterns (see pages 42–109).

TOOLS AND MATERIALS

One of the attractions of crochet snowflakes is that they do not require a large collection of specialised tools or materials. Select a steel hook and a ball of crochet thread, gather a few common household supplies and you'll be ready to begin.

CROCHET THREAD

Snowflakes are usually crocheted from cotton crochet thread, which comes in sizes from 3 to 100, with higher numbers indicating finer threads. Thicker threads are easiest to crochet, and for that reason, all of the patterns in this collection were designed for size 10 thread. Experiment with finer threads and smaller hooks to create smaller, lighter-weight snowflakes. You may also wish to try other materials, such as lace-weight yarns or embroidery floss, for beautiful and sometimes surprising results.

SCISSORS

A small, sharp-pointed pair of scissors is especially helpful for clipping thread ends.

CROCHET HOOKS

For crocheting in thread, you will need a small, steel crochet hook. The patterns in this book were developed using a 1.90mm (size 5) hook, but many charts recommend using a 1.65mm (size 7) or 1.5mm (size 8) crochet hook with size 10 thread. Thread thicknesses vary, as do the gauges of individual crocheters, so any hook size recommendation should be taken as a starting point only. For the purposes of these snowflakes, the correct hook to use is the one that allows you to work most comfortably with your chosen thread.

STARCH OR FABRIC STIFFENER

In order to hold their shapes, most snowflakes need to be stiffened. The material you use as a stiffener will depend on how you plan to use the snowflake, and on your personal preference. Laundry starch (either liquid starch, or heavy spray starch) can be used to stiffen snowflakes for hanging or for use as appliqués, while preserving the thread's soft, textile feel. Homemade sugar starches (recipes are available online) produce a similar effect. Commercial fabric stiffeners will give the snowflakes a hard or semi-hard finish, which can be useful for jewellery, hair accessories or hanging applications. (A mixture of PVA glue and water can be used as a substitute for fabric stiffener.)

STRAIGHT PINS

Use straight pins made from stainless steel, nickel-plated brass, or another rust-proof material, to hold your snowflake in position during blocking. It is a good idea to test the pins before use, to ensure that they won't stain your snowflakes. To do this, pin some to a piece of white fabric or a small crochet sample, dampen it with your choice of stiffener, let it dry and then check for rust spots or stains.

BLOCKING BOARD COMPONENTS

Snowflakes are best blocked on a blocking board, which can be made quickly and inexpensively, using readily available materials. You will need paper, tape, corrugated cardboard or cork board, cling film and the instructions on page 19.

PATTERNS AND ABBREVIATIONS

On these pages you will find information on the abbreviations, symbols and terminology used in the Snowflake patterns chapter (see pages 42–109), and elsewhere in this book.

ENGLISH/AMERICAN TERMINOLOGY

The patterns in this book use English terminology, which differs somewhat from American terminology. You may find this list of English terms and their American equivalents useful.

ENGLISH	AMERICAN
double crochet (**dc**)	single crochet (**sc**)
half treble (**htr**)	half double crochet (**hdc**)
treble (**tr**)	double crochet (**dc**)
double treble (**dtr**)	treble (**tr**)
triple treble (**trtr**)	double treble (**dtr**)

BASIC SYMBOLS AND ABBREVIATIONS

○	Chain	**ch**	Chain
●	Slip stitch	**ss**	Slip stitch
+	Double crochet	**dc**	Double crochet
T	Half treble crochet	**htr**	Half treble crochet
⊤	Treble crochet	**tr**	Treble crochet
⊤	Double treble	**dtr**	Double treble

INCREASES

Symbols joined at the base show stitches worked in a single stitch or space to make an increase. They are usually described as 'work so many stitches in the next stitch,' or at the beginning of a row 'work so many stitches in the stitch below'.

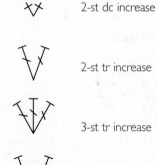

2-st dc increase

2-st tr increase

3-st tr increase

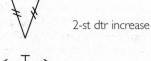

2-st dtr increase

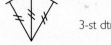

3-st dtr increase

ADDITIONAL PATTERN NOTES

In all of the patterns in this book, snowflake dimensions and thread yardage estimates assume the use of size 10 thread and a 1.90mm (size 5) hook.

Asterisks (* **) indicate material to be repeated, with starting and ending points:

• **Repeat from ***	*means:*	Repeat all instructions that you've been given, starting with the last *.
• **Repeat from * to ***	*means:*	Repeat the instructions between the last * and the ** that follows it.

In snowflakes, it is common for a group of stitches to be repeated several times, and then partially repeated again.

• **Repeat from * 4 times, and from * to ** once more**	*means:*	Repeat all instructions, starting at the last *, 4 times. Then begin a fifth repetition, but stop when you get to the **.

THE STRUCTURE OF SNOWFLAKES – CREATING YOUR OWN PATTERNS

If you reach a point where you've crocheted all of the designs and want to invent some of your own, here is some information that will help:

• All snowflakes have six symmetrical points, and most are crocheted in the round.

• To design a pattern from scratch, begin with a foundation ring large enough to accommodate the number of stitches in your first round: 4-chain rings are a good size to hold 5 stitches, and 6-chain rings are a good size to hold 11 stitches.

• The number of stitches in your first round (including the turning chain) should be a multiple of 6. In practice this usually means working a turning chain plus 5 stitches, or a turning chain

plus 11 stitches into the foundation ring. If you like, you can add lengths of chain between these stitches, to create points, loops or arms.

• Using your early rows to create a simple, 6-pointed base like a hexagon or a six-pointed star will allow the rest of the pattern to grow naturally into a snowflake. Build your design outwards by adding loops, clusters or other ornamentation around the points, keeping the pattern symmetrical.

• You may wish to begin with the first two or three rounds of one of the snowflakes in this book, and then finish with an outer edge of your own design. The Nor'easter series (see pages 53–54) and the other series snowflakes in this collection illustrate how various edgings can be used to turn a single base into many different snowflakes.

CROCHET REFRESHER COURSE

For readers who are new to crochet (and those who could use a review), this section provides instruction on the stitches used in this book, as well as information about blocking and finishing. If you've never crocheted before, start by working the stitches with a large crochet hook in medium-weight yarn. Once you are comfortable with them, switch to thread.

HOLDING THE HOOK AND YARN

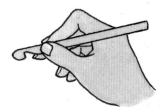

1 Holding the hook as if it were a pen is the most widely used method. Centre the tips of your right thumb and index finger over the flat section of the hook.

2 An alternative way to hold the hook is to grasp the flat section of the hook between your right thumb and index finger as if you were holding a knife.

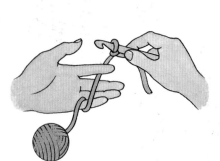

3 To control the supply and keep an even tension on the yarn, loop the short end of the yarn over your left index finger and take the yarn coming from the ball loosely around the little finger on the same hand. Use the middle finger on the same hand to help hold the work. If left-handed, hold the hook in the left hand and the yarn in the right.

MAKING A SLIP KNOT

1 Loop the yarn as shown, insert the hook into the loop, catch the yarn with the hook and pull it through to make a loop over the hook.

2 Gently pull the yarn to tighten the loop around the hook and complete the slip knot.

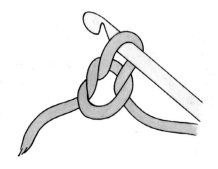

WORKING A FOUNDATION CHAIN (CH)

The foundation chain is the equivalent of casting on in knitting, and it's important to make sure that you have made the required number of chains for the pattern you are going to work. Count each V-shaped loop on the front of the chain as one chain stitch, except for the loop on the hook, which is not counted. You may find it easier to turn the chain over and count the stitches on the back of the chain. When working the first row of stitches (usually called the foundation row) into the chain, insert the hook under one thread or two, depending on your preference.

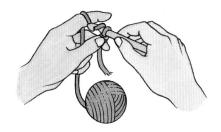

1 Holding the hook with the slip knot in your right hand and the yarn in your left, wrap the yarn over the hook. Draw the yarn through to make a new loop and complete the first chain stitch.

2 Repeat this step, drawing a new loop of yarn through the loop already on the hook until the chain is the required length. Move the thumb and index finger that are grasping the chain upwards after every few stitches to keep the tension even. When working into the chain, insert the hook under one thread (for a looser edge) or two (for a firmer edge), depending on your preference.

WORKING A SLIP STITCH (SL ST)

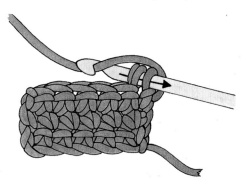

Slip stitch is the shortest of all the crochet stitches and its main uses are for joining rounds, making seams and carrying the hook and yarn from one place to another. Insert the hook from front to back into the required stitch. Wrap the yarn over the hook (*yarn over*) and draw it through both the work and the loop on the hook. One loop remains on the hook and one slip stitch has been worked.

WORKING A DOUBLE CROCHET (DC)

1 Begin with a foundation chain (see page 15) and insert the hook from front to back into the second chain from the hook. Wrap the yarn over the hook (*yarn over*) and draw it through the first loop, leaving two loops on the hook.

2 To complete the stitch, yarn over and draw it through both loops on the hook, leaving one loop on the hook. Continue in this way, working one double crochet into each chain.

3 At the end of the row, turn and work one chain for the turning chain (remember that this chain does not count as a stitch). Insert the hook into the first double crochet at the beginning of the row. Work a double crochet into each stitch of the previous row, being careful to work the final stitch into the last stitch of the row, but not into the turning chain.

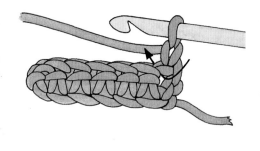

WORKING A HALF TREBLE (HTR)

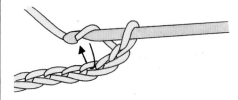

1 Begin with a foundation chain (see page 15), wrap the yarn over the hook (*yarn over*) and insert the hook into the third chain from the hook.

2 Draw the yarn through the chain, leaving three loops on the hook. Yarn over and draw through all three loops on the hook, leaving one loop on the hook. One half treble stitch is complete.

3 Continue along the row, working one half treble into each chain. At the end of the row, work two chains to turn. Skip the first stitch and work a half treble into each stitch made on the previous row. At the end of the row, work the last stitch into the top of the turning chain.

WORKING A TREBLE (TR)

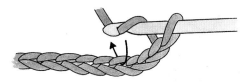

1 Begin with a foundation chain (see page 15), wrap the yarn over the hook and insert the hook into the fourth chain from the hook.

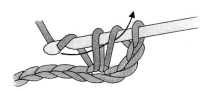

2 Draw the yarn through the chain, leaving three loops on the hook. Yarn over again and draw the yarn through the first two loops on the hook, leaving two loops on the hook.

3 Yarn over and draw the yarn through the two loops on the hook leaving one loop on the hook. One treble is complete. Continue along the row, working one treble stitch into each chain. At the end of the row, work three chains to turn. Skip the first stitch and work a treble into each stitch made on the previous row. At the end of the row, work the last stitch into the top of the turning chain.

WORKING A DOUBLE TREBLE (DTR)

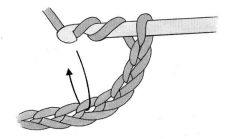

1 Begin with a foundation chain (see page 15), wrap the yarn over the hook twice (*yarn over twice*), and insert the hook into the fifth chain from the hook.

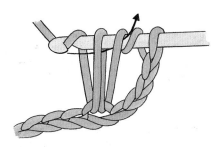

2 Draw the yarn through the chain, leaving four loops on the hook. Yarn over again and draw the yarn through the first two loops on the hook, leaving three loops on the hook.

3 Yarn over again and draw through the first two loops on the hook leaving two loops on the hook.

4 Yarn over again and draw through the two remaining loops, leaving one loop on the hook. Double treble is now complete.

5 Continue along the row, working one double treble stitch into each chain. At the end of the row, work four chains to turn. Skip the first stitch and work a double treble into each stitch made on the previous row. At the end of the row, work the last stitch into the top of the turning chain.

WORKING IN ROUNDS

Snowflakes are worked in rounds, which means that they are worked outwards from a central ring called a foundation ring.

MAKING A FOUNDATION RING

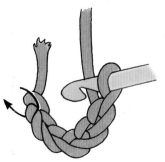

Work a short length of foundation chain (see page 15) as specified in the pattern. Join the chains into a ring by working a slip stitch into the first stitch of the foundation chain.

WORKING INTO THE RING

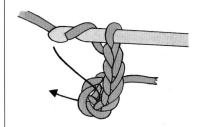

1 Work the number of turning chains specified in the pattern – three chains are shown here (counting as a treble stitch). Inserting the hook into the space at the center of the ring each time, work the number of stitches specified in the pattern into the ring. Count the stitches at the end of the round to check you have worked the correct number.

2 Join the first and last stitches of the round together by working a slip stitch into the top of the turning chain.

FINISHING OFF THE FINAL ROUND

To make a neat edge, finish off the final round by using this method of sewing the first and last stitches together in preference to the slip stitch joining method shown above.

1 Cut the yarn, leaving an end of about 10cm (4in) and draw it through the last stitch. With right side facing, thread the end in a large tapestry needle and take it under both loops of the stitch next to the turning chain.

2 Pull the needle through and insert it into the centre of the last stitch of the round. On the wrong side, pull the needle through to complete the stitch, adjust the length of the stitch to close the round, then weave in the end on the wrong side in the usual way.

BLOCKING AND STIFFENING

To make your snowflake flat, neat and symmetrical (and to ensure that it stays that way during hanging), it is necessary to block and stiffen it.

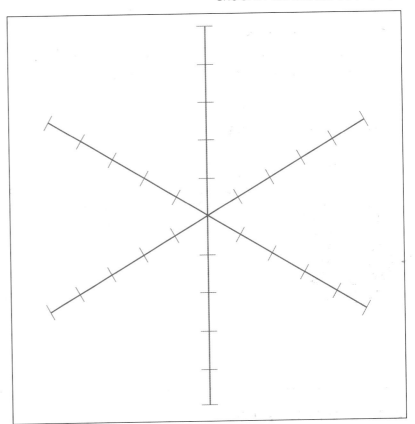

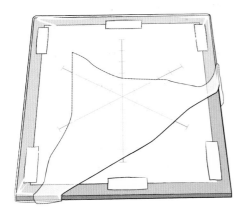

1 Make a blocking board. Copy or trace the blocking diagram shown here onto a sheet of paper, and tape it to a flat piece of corrugated cardboard, cork board or any other rigid, pin-friendly material, such as polystyrene. Then cover it with cling film, so that it will be waterproof.

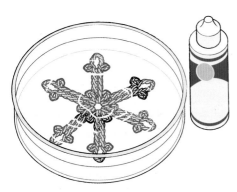

2 Soak the snowflake with heavy laundry starch, fabric stiffener or (for applications that do not require a stiff snowflake) water. Gently squeeze out any excess liquid, and press the snowflake approximately to shape.

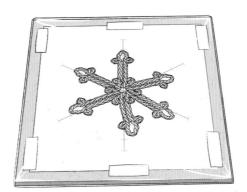

3 Lay the snowflake on the blocking board, on the centre of the blocking diagram. Use the diagram's lines as guides to aid in symmetrical placement of the snowflake's arms, and adjust the snowflake until it is flat and even, with straight arms and neat loops.

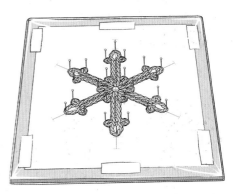

4 Secure the snowflake to the board with straight pins. Let it dry completely before removing it.

SNOWFLAKE SHOWCASE

Browse this lacy showcase of the featured snowflake designs to find the ones that most catch your eye. When you've selected one to crochet, turn to the Snowflake patterns (see pages 42–109) for full instructions.

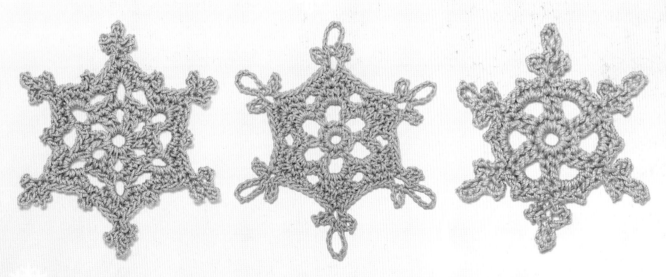

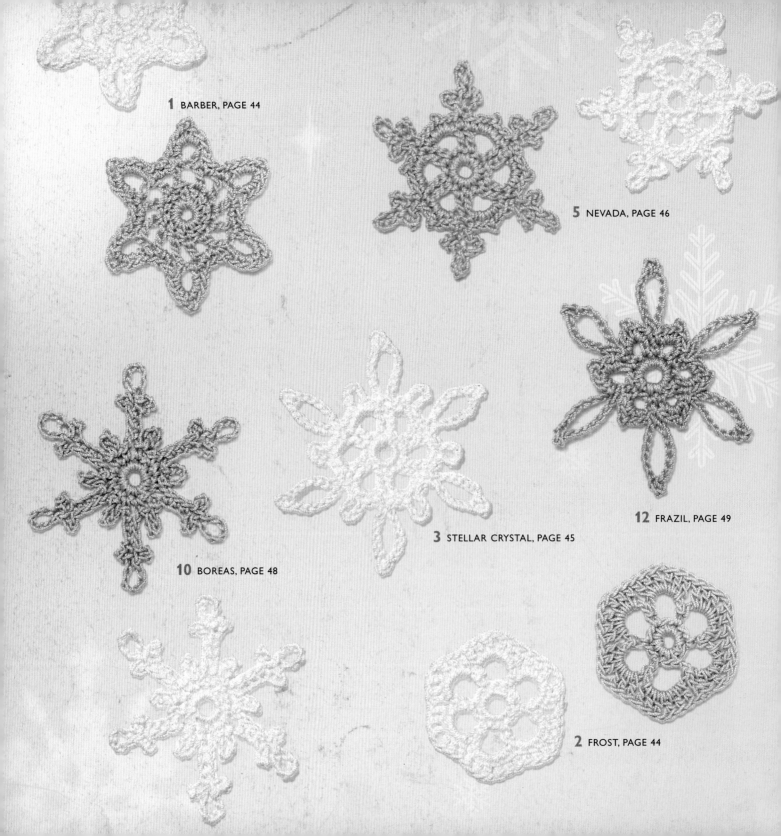

1 BARBER, PAGE 44

5 NEVADA, PAGE 46

12 FRAZIL, PAGE 49

3 STELLAR CRYSTAL, PAGE 45

10 BOREAS, PAGE 48

2 FROST, PAGE 44

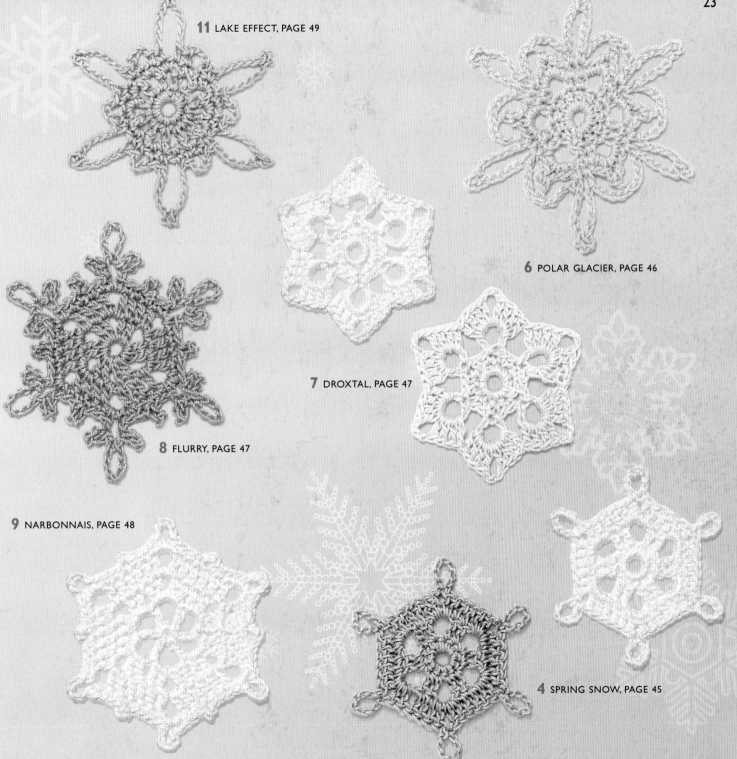

11 LAKE EFFECT, PAGE 49

6 POLAR GLACIER, PAGE 46

7 DROXTAL, PAGE 47

8 FLURRY, PAGE 47

9 NARBONNAIS, PAGE 48

4 SPRING SNOW, PAGE 45

16 ARCTIC MIST, PAGE 51

23 FIRN, PAGE 55

13 SNOW MIST, PAGE 50

14 SIKUSSAK, PAGE 50

21 NOR'EASTER III, PAGE 54

15 WHITE BURAN, PAGE 51

17 KOSSAVA, PAGE 52

20 NOR'EASTER II, PAGE 53

18 ICE FLOWER, PAGE 52

19 NOR'EASTER 1, PAGE 53

24 KAAVIE, PAGE 55

22 NOR'EASTER IV, PAGE 54

30 ICE CRYSTAL II, PAGE 59

31 SQUALL, PAGE 60

27 FIRNSPIEGEL, PAGE 57

28 NORTE, PAGE 58

29 ICE CRYSTAL I, PAGE 58

26 AUVERGNASSE, PAGE 56

34 NORTHER, PAGE 61

33 CAVABURD, PAGE 61

32 FROST MIST, PAGE 60

25 ICE PRISM, PAGE 56

35 HALO, PAGE 62

36 BORA, PAGE 62

45 AUFEIS I, PAGE 68

37 NIEVE PENITENTE, PAGE 63

39 KAIKIAS, PAGE 64

38 THUNDERSNOW, PAGE 64

42 TAKU, PAGE 66

44 BISE NOIR, PAGE 68

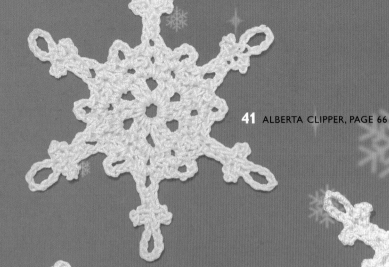

41 ALBERTA CLIPPER, PAGE 66

43 ALPINE GLACIER, PAGE 67

47 SLEET 1, PAGE 70

40 SILVER FROST, PAGE 65

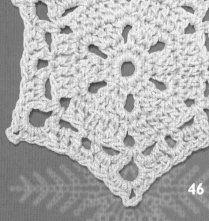

46 AUFEIS II, PAGE 69

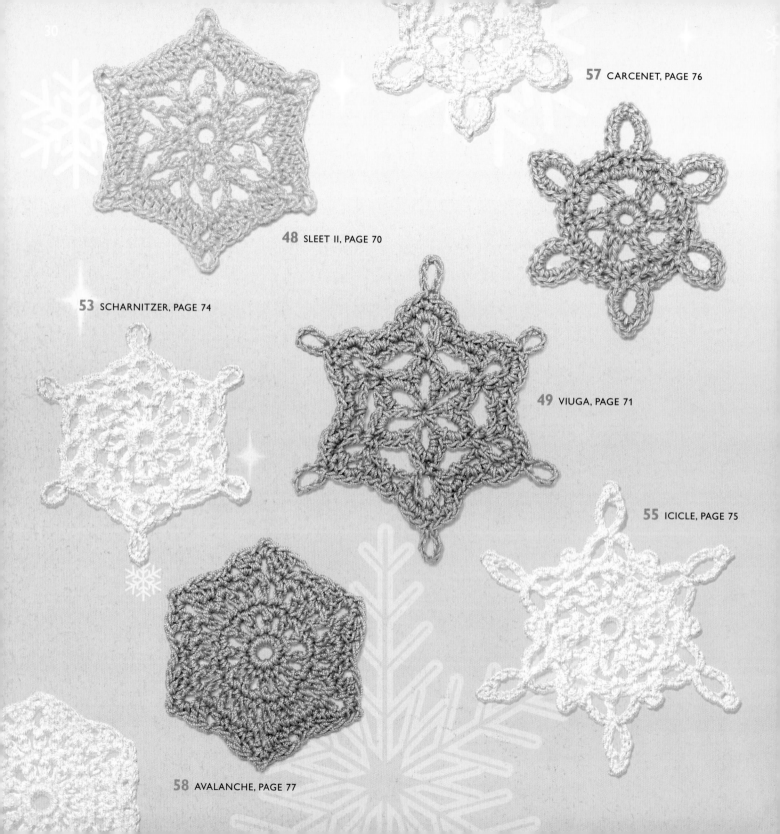

57 CARCENET, PAGE 76

48 SLEET II, PAGE 70

53 SCHARNITZER, PAGE 74

49 VIUGA, PAGE 71

55 ICICLE, PAGE 75

58 AVALANCHE, PAGE 77

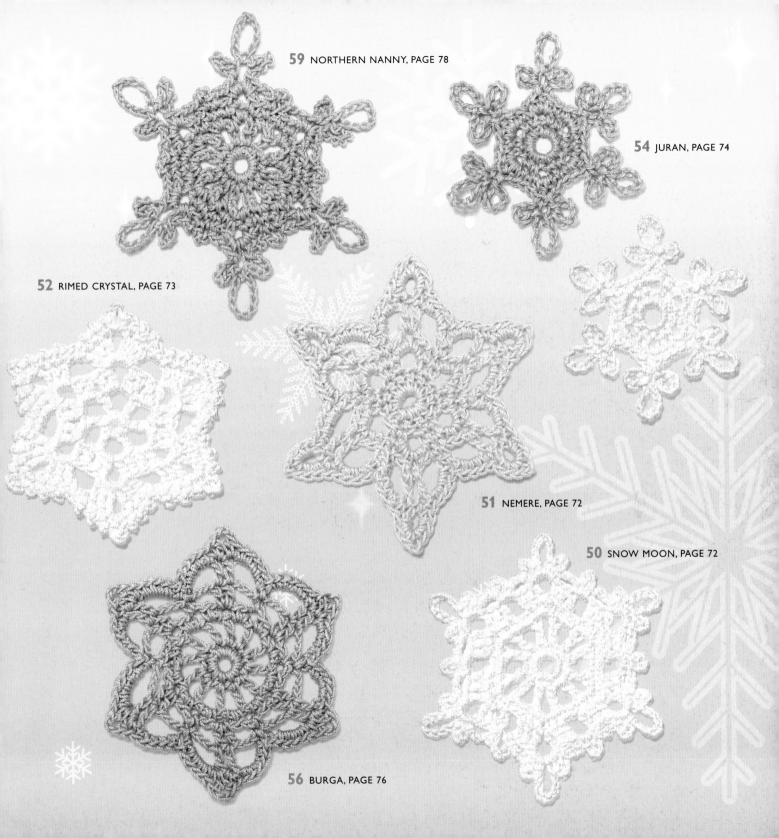

59 NORTHERN NANNY, PAGE 78

54 JURAN, PAGE 74

52 RIMED CRYSTAL, PAGE 73

51 NEMERE, PAGE 72

50 SNOW MOON, PAGE 72

56 BURGA, PAGE 76

65 SEA ICE I, PAGE 82

64 ELVEGUST, PAGE 81

68 CANDLE ICE, PAGE 84

67 N'ASCHI, PAGE 83

60 MISTRAL, PAGE 78

69 PLANE DENDRITE, PAGE 84

61 CIRQUE GLACIER, PAGE 79

62 WINTER SOLSTICE, PAGE 80

63 SUESTADA, PAGE 80

66 SEA ICE II, PAGE 82

70 WHITEOUT, PAGE 85

74 BLIZZARD, PAGE 88

76 POLARIS, PAGE 89

72 CIERZO, PAGE 86

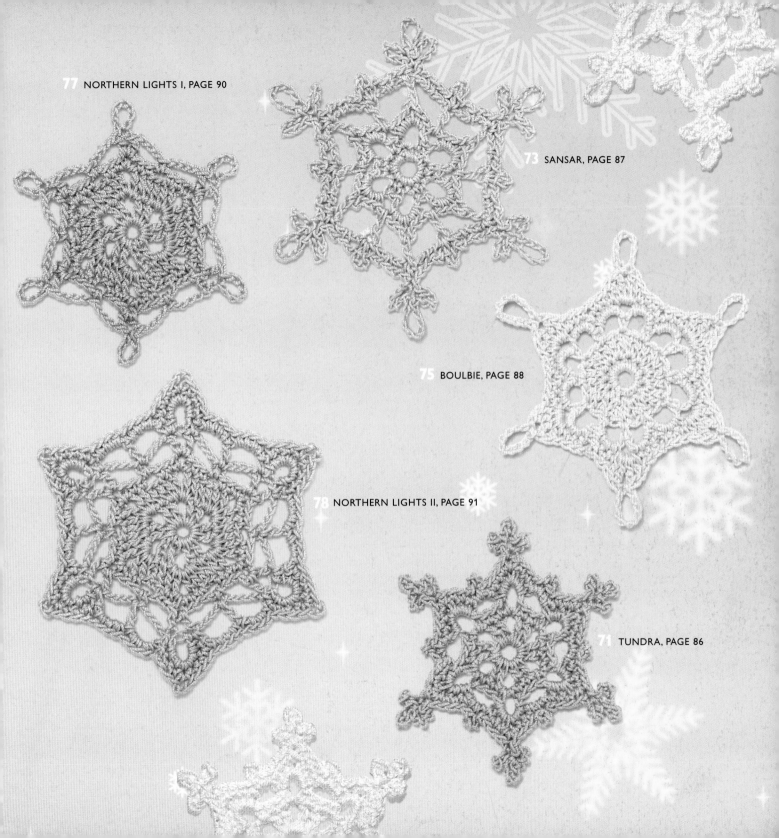

77 NORTHERN LIGHTS I, PAGE 90

73 SANSAR, PAGE 87

75 BOULBIE, PAGE 88

78 NORTHERN LIGHTS II, PAGE 91

71 TUNDRA, PAGE 86

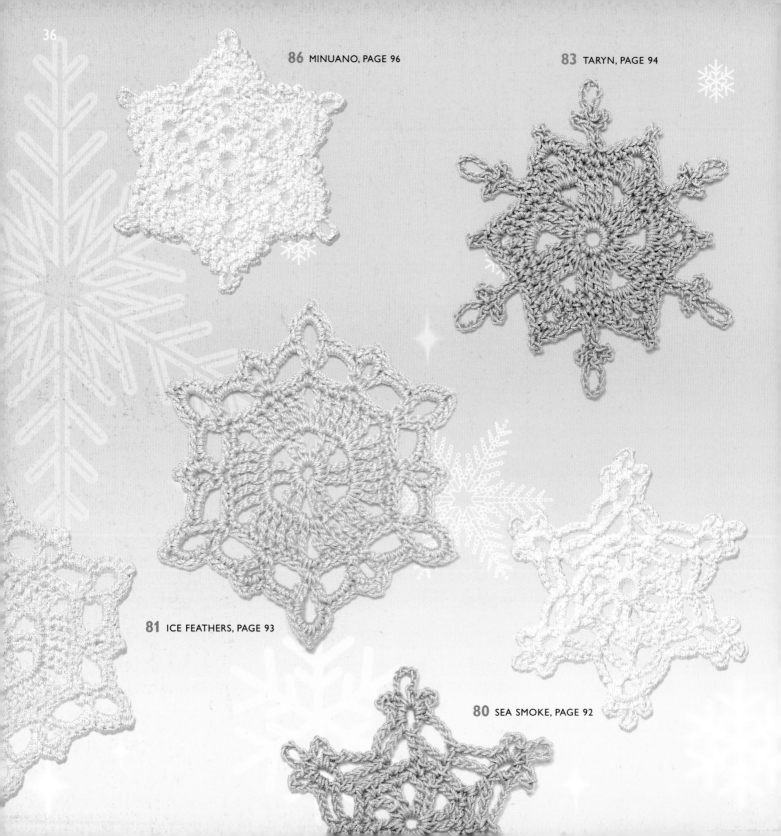

86 MINUANO, PAGE 96

83 TARYN, PAGE 94

81 ICE FEATHERS, PAGE 93

80 SEA SMOKE, PAGE 92

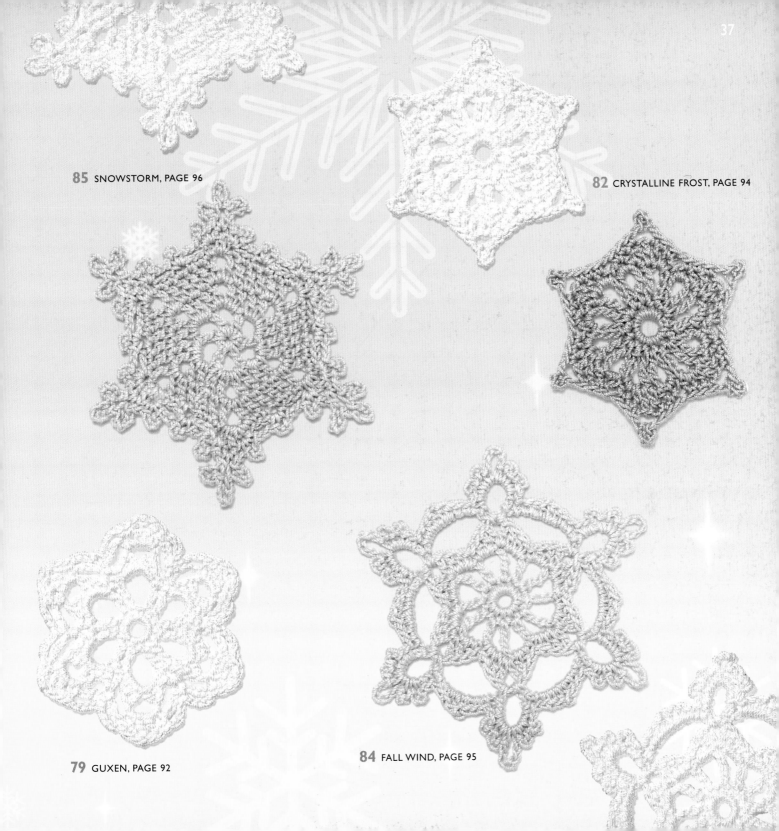

85 SNOWSTORM, PAGE 96

82 CRYSTALLINE FROST, PAGE 94

79 GUXEN, PAGE 92

84 FALL WIND, PAGE 95

91 CRIVETZ, PAGE 100

89 SNOWDRIFT, PAGE 99

94 BURIA, PAGE 103

92 PERMAFROST, PAGE 101

87 GALLEGO, PAGE 97

90 WHITE DEW, PAGE 100

88 AUTAN NOIR, PAGE 98

93 ICE FRONT, PAGE 102

40

97 FLANDERS STORM, PAGE 106

98 BLUE ICE, PAGE 107

95 GRAUPEL, PAGE 104

96 NÉVÉ, PAGE 105

100 AUSTRU, PAGE 109

99 GALE, PAGE 108

SNOWFLAKE PATTERNS

Organised by level of difficulty, this chapter contains patterns and charts for all of the snowflakes featured in this book. Use it in conjunction with the Snowflake showcase (see pages 20–41), or work through it from the beginning, increasing your skills as you go.

1 BARBER
See page 22 in the showcase

This small, sharp-edged flake is named after the Barber, a blizzard of snow and ice in the Gulf of St. Lawrence.

Finished diameter: 54mm (2⅛in)
Thread required: 4.6m (5yd)

Foundation ring: ch 6; join with sl st in first ch.
Rnd 1: ch 3 (counts as tr). 11 tr in ring; join with sl st in 3rd ch of initial ch 3.
Rnd 2: ch 3 (counts as tr). *ch 1. tr in 1 tr. ch 8, and sl st in 8th ch from hook to form loop.** tr in next tr. Repeat from * 4 times, and from * to ** once more. Join with sl st in 3rd ch of initial ch 3.
Rnd 3: ch 1 (counts as dc). *dc in ch 1 space. dc in tr. ch 1. [3 dc, ch 3, 3 dc] in ch 8 loop. ch 1.** dc in next tr. Repeat from * 4 times, and from * to ** once more. Join with sl st in initial ch 1. Finish off; weave in ends.

2 FROST
See page 22 in the showcase

You might find ice crystals like this one decorating your window on a late autumn morning.

Finished diameter: 44mm (1¾in)
Thread required: 3.7m (4yd)

Foundation ring: ch 6; join with sl st in first ch.
Rnd 1: ch 1 (counts as dc). 11 dc in ring; join with sl st in initial ch 1.
Rnd 2: ch 1 (counts as dc). *ch 7. Skip 1 dc, and dc in 1 dc. Repeat from * 4 times. ch 7. Join with sl st in initial ch 1.
Rnd 3: sl st in next ch 7 space. ch 3 (counts as tr). In same ch 7 space work: 2 tr, ch 1, 3 tr. [3 tr, ch 1, 3 tr] in each of the 5 remaining ch 7 spaces. Join with sl st in 3rd ch of initial ch 3. Finish off; weave in ends.

3	STELLAR CRYSTAL

See page 22 in the showcase

A stellar crystal is a flat, star-shaped ice crystal; in other words, a perfect snowflake!

Finished diameter: 73mm (2⅞in)
Thread required: 4.6m (5yd)

Foundation ring: ch 6; join with sl st in first ch.
Rnd 1: ch 1 (counts as dc). 11 dc in ring; join with sl st in initial ch 1.
Rnd 2: ch 3 (counts as tr). tr in 1 dc. *ch 3. tr in 2 dc. Repeat from * 4 times. ch 3. Join with sl st in 3rd ch of initial ch 3.
Rnd 3: ch 1 (counts as dc). *ch 11, and sl st in 4th ch from hook to form picot. ch 6, and sl st in 1st ch of ch 11. dc in next tr. [2 dc, ch 6, 2 dc] in ch 3 space (to form loop).** dc in 1 tr. Repeat from * 4 times, and from * to ** once more. Join with sl st in initial ch 1. Finish off; weave in ends.

4	SPRING SNOW

See page 23 in the showcase

Spring snow is a wet, granular snow. As its name suggests, it is usually found in the spring.

Finished diameter: 60mm (2⅜in)
Thread required: 4.6m (5yd)

Foundation ring: ch 6; join with sl st in first ch.
Rnd 1: ch 1 (counts as dc). 11 dc in ring; join with sl st in initial ch 1.
Rnd 2: ch 3 (counts as tr). tr in 1 dc. *ch 3. tr in 2 dc. Repeat from * 4 times. ch 3. Join with sl st in 3rd ch of initial ch 3.
Rnd 3: ch 3 (counts as tr). tr in tr. *2 tr in ch 3 space. ch 8, and sl st in 8th ch from hook to form loop. 2 tr in same ch 3 space as last tr.** tr in 2 tr. Repeat from * 4 times, and from * to ** once more. Join with sl st in 3rd ch of initial ch 3. Finish off; weave in ends.

SKILL LEVEL BEGINNER

SKILL LEVEL BEGINNER

5 NEVADA
See page 22 in the showcase

This pretty snowflake might have been carried down on a Nevada, a cold wind blowing from a mountain glacier.

Finished diameter: 57mm (2¼in)
Thread required: 4.6m (5yd)

Foundation ring: ch 6; join with sl st in first ch.
Rnd 1: ch 1 (counts as dc). 11 dc in ring; join with sl st in initial ch 1.
Rnd 2: ch 3 (counts as tr). tr in 1 dc. *ch 3. tr in 2 dc. Repeat from * 4 times. ch 3. Join with sl st in 3rd ch of ch 3.
Rnd 3: ch 1 (counts as dc). *ch 5, and sl st in 4th ch from hook to form picot. ch 6, and sl st in 6th ch from hook. ch 4, and sl st in 4th ch from hook. sl st in 1st ch of ch 5. dc in next tr. [2 dc, ch 2, 2 dc] in ch 3 space.** dc in 1 tr. Repeat from * 4 times, and from * to ** once more. Join with sl st in initial ch 1. Finish off; weave in ends.

6 POLAR GLACIER
See page 23 in the showcase

This airy flake is much less complicated than it looks; it is an inner hexagon decorated with a series of chains and picots.

Finished diameter: 70mm (2¾in)
Thread required: 5.5m (6yd)

Foundation ring: ch 6; join with sl st in first ch.
Rnd 1: ch 3 (counts as tr). 11 tr in ring; join with sl st in 3rd ch of initial ch 3.
Rnd 2: ch 1 (counts as dc). dc in 1 tr. *ch 4. dc in 2 tr. Repeat from * 4 times. ch 4. Join with sl st in initial ch 1.
Rnd 3: ch 1 (counts as dc). dc in dc. *[2 dc, ch 3, 2 dc] in ch 4 space.** dc in 2 dc. Repeat from * 4 times, and from * to ** once more. Join with sl st in initial ch 1.
Rnd 4: ch 1 (counts as dc). *ch 9, and sl st in 4th ch from hook to form picot. ch 5. dc in next dc. ch 4. tr in next ch 3 point. ch 4.** Skip 2 dc, and dc in 1 dc. Repeat from * 4 times, and from * to ** once more. Join with sl st in initial ch 1. Finish off; weave in ends.

7 DROXTAL
See page 23 in the showcase

This simple design is named after droxtals, tiny ice particles formed from fine water droplets.

Finished diameter: 44mm (1¾in)
Thread required: 4.6m (5yd)

Foundation ring: ch 6; join with sl st in first ch.
Rnd 1: ch 1 (counts as first dc). 11 dc in ring; join with sl st in initial ch 1.
Rnd 2: ch 1 (counts as first dc). dc in 1 dc. *ch 8, and sl st in 8th ch from hook to form loop.** dc in 2 dc. Repeat from * 4 times, and from * to ** once more. Join with sl st in initial ch 1.
Rnd 3: sl st in dc, and in first 2 ch of ch 8 loop. sl st in loop, and ch 3 (counts as tr). 3 tr in loop, ch 3, and 4 tr in same loop. [4 tr, ch 3, 4 tr] in each of the 5 remaining ch 8 loops. Join with sl st in 3rd ch of initial ch 3. Finish off; weave in ends.

8 FLURRY
See page 23 in the showcase

This flake would fit perfectly with the others floating down in an early winter snow flurry.

Finished diameter: 64mm (2½in)
Thread required: 5.5m (6yd)

Foundation ring: ch 6; join with sl st in first ch.
Rnd 1: ch 3 (counts as tr). 1 tr in ring. *ch 2; 2 tr in ring. Repeat from * 4 times. ch 2. Join with sl st in 3rd ch of initial ch 3.
Rnd 2: ch 3 (counts as tr). tr in 1 tr. *[tr, ch 2, tr] in ch 2 point.** tr in 2 tr. Repeat from * 4 times, and from * to ** once more. Join with sl st in 3rd ch of initial ch 3.
Rnd 3: ch 1 (counts as dc). *ch 4, and sl st in 4th ch from hook to make picot. dc in next 2 tr. dc in ch 2 point. ch 6, and sl st in 6th ch from hook. ch 8, and sl st in 8th ch from hook. ch 6, and sl st in 6th ch from hook. dc in same ch 2 space as last dc.** dc in 2 tr. Repeat from * 4 times, and from * to ** once more. dc in tr. Join with sl st in initial ch 1. Finish off; weave in ends.

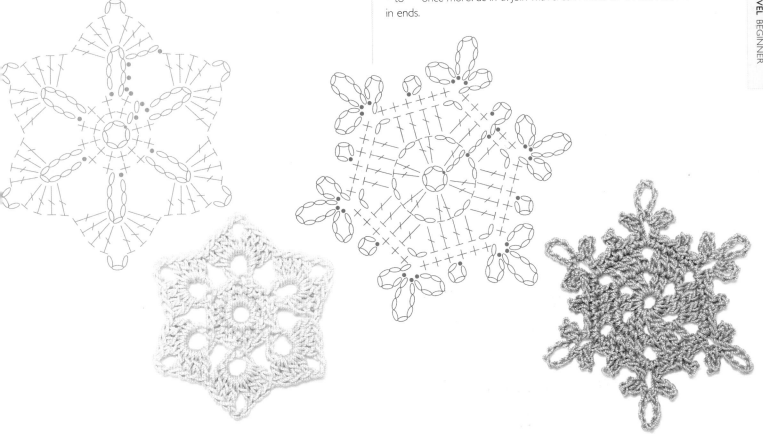

9 NARBONNAIS
See page 23 in the showcase

This snowflake takes its name from the Narbonnais, a sometimes-stormy winter wind in France.

Finished diameter: 64mm (2½in)
Thread required: 6.4m (7yd)

Foundation ring: ch 4; join with sl st in first ch.
Rnd 1: ch 3 (counts as tr). *ch 3. tr in ring. Repeat from * 4 times. ch 3, and join in 3rd ch of initial ch 3.
Rnd 2: sl st in ch 3 space. ch 3 (counts as tr). tr in same space. ch 2; 2 tr in same ch 3 space. [2 tr; ch 2, 2 tr] in each of the 5 remaining ch 3 spaces. Join with sl st in 3rd ch of initial ch 3.
Rnd 3: ch 3 (counts as tr). tr in tr. *[tr; ch 2, tr] in ch 2 point.** tr in 4 tr. Repeat from * 4 times, and from * to ** once more. tr in next 2 tr. Join in 3rd ch of initial ch 3.
Rnd 4: ch 1 (counts as dc). dc in 2 tr. *[2 dc, ch 5, 2 dc] in ch 2 point. dc in 3 tr. ch 3.** dc in next 3 tr. Repeat from * 4 times, and from * to ** once more. Join with sl st in initial ch 1. Finish off; weave in ends.

10 BOREAS
See page 22 in the showcase

Boreas was the ancient Greek name for the cold north wind, and a fitting title for this icy crystal.

Finished diameter: 60mm (2⅜in)
Thread required: 3.7m (4yd)

Foundation ring: ch 6; join with sl st in first ch.
Rnd 1: ch 1 (counts as dc). 11 dc in ring; join with sl st in initial ch 1.
Rnd 2: ch 1 (counts as dc). *ch 8, and sl st in 4th ch from hook to form picot. ch 7, and sl st in 7th ch from hook. ch 4, and sl st in 4th ch from hook. dc in 4th, 3rd, and 2nd ch of the ch 8. ch 1. Skip 1 ch; dc in next dc on the main ring. ch 6, and sl st in 6th ch from hook.** dc in next dc. Repeat from * 4 times, and from * to ** once more. Join with sl st in initial ch 1. Finish off; weave in ends.

11 LAKE EFFECT
See page 23 in the showcase

The winter wind blowing over the Great Lakes can bring rafts of shivery flakes like this one.

Finished diameter: 64mm (2½in)
Thread required: 4.6m (5yd)

Foundation ring: ch 6; join with sl st in first ch.
Rnd 1: ch 1 (counts as dc). 11 dc in ring; join with sl st in initial ch 1.
Rnd 2: ch 1 (counts as dc). *ch 3. dc in next dc. Repeat from * 10 times. ch 3. Join with sl st in initial ch 1.
Rnd 3: sl st in next ch 3 space. ch 1 (counts as dc), and dc in same ch 3 space. 2 dc in each of the 11 remaining ch 3 spaces. Join with sl st in initial ch 1.
Rnd 4: ch 1 (counts as dc). *ch 4. dc in next 2 dc. ch 8, and join with sl st in 3rd ch from hook to form picot. ch 5.** dc in next 2 dc. Repeat from * 4 times, and from * to ** once more. dc in next dc. Join with sl st in initial ch 1. Finish off; weave in ends.

12 FRAZIL
See page 22 in the showcase

Frazil is a type of flowing ice that forms in turbulent water.

Finished diameter: 64mm (2½in)
Thread required: 3.7m (4yd)

Foundation ring: ch 6; join with sl st in first ch.
Rnd 1: ch 1 (counts as dc). 11 dc in ring; join with sl st in initial ch 1.
Rnd 2: ch 1 (counts as dc). dc in 1 dc. *ch 3. dc in 2 dc. Repeat from * 4 times. ch 3. Join with sl st in initial ch 1.
Rnd 3: *ch 10, and sl st in 3rd ch from hook to form picot. ch 7. sl st in next dc. [2 dc, ch 2, 2dc] in next ch 3 space.** sl st in next dc. Repeat from * 4 times, and from * to ** once more. Join with sl st in sl st. Finish off; weave in ends.

SKILL LEVEL: BEGINNER

13 **SNOW MIST**
See page 24 in the showcase

This little star might have fallen in a mist of tiny ice crystals.

Finished diameter: 60mm (2⅜in)
Thread required: 5.5m (6yd)

Foundation ring: ch 6; join with sl st in first ch.
Rnd 1: ch 1 (counts as dc). 11 dc in ring; join with sl st in initial ch 1.
Rnd 2: ch 1 (counts as dc). dc in 1 dc. *ch 4. dc in 2 dc. Repeat from * 4 times. ch 4. Join with sl st in initial ch 1.
Rnd 3: sl st in dc, and in ch 4 point. ch 1 (counts as dc). dc in same ch 4 point. ch 4, and 2 dc in same point. *ch 2. [2 dc, ch 4, 2 dc] in next ch 4 point. Repeat from * 4 times. ch 2. Join with sl st in initial ch 1.
Rnd 4: ch 1 (counts as dc). dc in dc. *[2 dc, ch 6, 2 dc] in ch 4 point. dc in 2 dc. 1 dc in ch 2 space.** dc in next 2 dc. Repeat from * 4 times, and from * to ** once more. Join with sl st in initial ch 1. Finish off; weave in ends.

14 **SIKUSSAK**
See page 24 in the showcase

This lovely, flower-centered flake takes its name from a Greenlandic word for old sea ice trapped in fjords.

Finished diameter: 57mm (2¼in)
Thread required: 5.5m (6yd)

Foundation ring: ch 4; join with sl st in first ch.
Rnd 1: ch 1 (counts as first dc), *ch 8, dc in ring to form loop. Repeat from * 4 times. ch 8. Join with sl st in initial ch 1.
Rnd 2: sl st in first 2 ch of first ch 8 loop. sl st inside the loop, and ch 1 (counts as first dc). 3 dc in loop. *ch 2. 4 dc in next loop. Repeat from * 4 times. ch 2. Join with sl st in initial ch 1.
Rnd 3: ch 1 (counts as first dc). dc in 1 dc. ch 2, and dc in next 2 dc. *2 dc in ch 2 space. dc in 2 dc. ch 2, and dc in next 2 dc. Repeat from * 4 times. 2 dc in ch 2 space. Join with sl st in initial ch 1.
Rnd 4: ch 1 (counts as first dc), dc in dc. *[dc, ch 6, dc] in ch 2 space.** dc in 6 dc. Repeat from * 4 times, and from * to ** once more. dc in 4 dc. Join with sl st in initial ch 1. Finish off; weave in ends.

15 WHITE BURAN
See page 24 in the showcase

The Buran is a strong northeast wind in central Asia. In the wintertime, it lifts snow from the ground, creating blizzard conditions and earning the name White Buran.

Finished diameter: 70mm (2¾in)
Thread required: 5.5m (6yd)

Foundation ring: ch 6; join with sl st in first ch.
Rnd 1: ch 1 (counts as first dc). 11 dc in ring; join with sl st in initial ch 1.
Rnd 2: ch 1 (counts as dc). dc in 1 dc. *ch 5. dc in 2 dc. Repeat from * 4 times. ch 5. Join with sl st in initial ch 1.
Rnd 3: ch 3 (counts as tr). tr in dc. *ch 2. dc in ch 5 point. ch 2.** tr in 2 dc. Repeat from * 4 times, and from * to ** once more. Join with sl st in 3rd ch of initial ch 3.
Rnd 4: ch 1 (counts as dc). dc in tr. *2 dc in ch 2 space. dc in dc. ch 7, and sl st in 6th ch from hook to form loop. ch 8, and sl st in 8th ch from hook. ch 6, and sl st in 6th ch from hook. sl st in 1st ch of ch 7. dc in same dc as last dc. 2 dc in next ch 2 space.** dc in 2 tr. Repeat from * 4 times, and from * to ** once more. Join with sl st in initial ch 1. Finish off; weave in ends.

16 ARCTIC MIST
See page 24 in the showcase

Also called ice fog, arctic mist is a fog of minute ice particles, suspended in the air.

Finished diameter: 60mm (2⅜in)
Thread required: 5.5m (6yd)

Foundation ring: ch 6; join with sl st in first ch.
Rnd 1: ch 1 (counts as dc). 11 dc in ring; join with sl st in initial ch 1.
Rnd 2: ch 3 (counts as tr). tr in 1 dc. *ch 3. tr in 2 dc. Repeat from * 4 times. ch 3. Join with sl st in 3rd ch of initial ch 3.
Rnd 3: ch 3 (counts as tr). *ch 2. tr in next tr. [2 tr, ch 6, 2 tr] in ch 3 space.** tr in 1 tr. Repeat from * 4 times, and from * to ** once more. Join with sl st in 3rd ch of initial ch 3.
Rnd 4: sl st in ch 2 point, and ch 1 (counts as dc). *ch 3. [2 dc, ch 2, 2 dc] in top of next ch 6 loop. ch 3.** dc in next ch 2 point (halfway between loops). Repeat from * 4 times, and from * to ** once more. Join with sl st in initial ch 1. Finish off; weave in ends.

17 KOSSAVA
See page 25 in the showcase

Chains and loops decorate this lacy snowflake, which is named after a cold, squally wind that blows from the Danube region.

Finished diameter: 67mm (2⅝in)
Thread required: 4.6m (5yd)

Foundation ring: ch 6; join with sl st in first ch.
Rnd 1: ch 3 (counts as tr). 1 tr in ring. *ch 2. 2 tr in ring. Repeat from * 4 times. ch 2. Join with sl st in 3rd ch of initial ch 3.
Rnd 2: ch 1 (counts as dc). dc in tr. *[dc, ch 4, dc] in ch 2 space.** dc in 2 tr. Repeat from * 4 times, and from * to ** once more. Join with sl st in initial ch 1.
Rnd 3: sl st in 2 dc, and in ch 4 point. ch 1 (counts as dc). dc in same point. *ch 6, and sl st in 6th ch from hook to form loop. ch 8, and sl st in 8th ch from hook. ch 6, and sl st in 6th ch from hook. 2 dc in same ch 4 point as last dc. ch 4.** 2 dc in next ch 4 point. Repeat from * 4 times, and from * to ** once more. Join with sl st in initial ch 1. Finish off; weave in ends.

18 ICE FLOWER
See page 25 in the showcase

This snowflake's dense pattern of stitching is reminiscent of ice flowers, thick and delicate clusters of frost.

Finished diameter: 60mm (2⅜in)
Thread required: 5.5m (6yd)

Foundation ring: ch 6; join with sl st in first ch.
Rnd 1: ch 1 (counts as dc). 11 dc in ring; join with sl st in initial ch 1.
Rnd 2: ch 1 (counts as dc). dc in 1 dc. *ch 4. dc in 2 dc. Repeat from * 4 times. ch 4. Join with sl st in initial ch 1.
Rnd 3: ch 1 (counts as dc). dc in dc. *[2 dc, ch 4, 2 dc] in ch 4 space.** dc in 2 dc. Repeat from * 4 times, and from * to ** once more. Join with sl st in initial ch 1.
Rnd 4: ch 1 (counts as dc). *ch 3. dc in next 2 dc. ch 1. Skip 1 dc; [dc, ch 6, dc, ch 8, dc, ch 6, dc] in ch 4 space. ch 1.** Skip 1 dc; dc in 2 dc. Repeat from * 4 times, and from * to ** once more. Skip 1 dc, and dc in 1 dc. Join with sl st in initial ch 1. Finish off; weave in ends.

19 NOR'EASTER I
See page 25 in the showcase

The Nor'easter series demonstrates some of the ways in which any six-sided base can be finished with different trims to create an almost endless variety of snowflakes. Nor'easter I begins the series with a double-crocheted border, and simple loops at the points.

Finished diameter: 60mm (2⅜in)
Thread required: 5.5m (6yd)

Foundation ring: ch 6; join with sl st in first ch.
Rnd 1: ch 1 (counts as dc). 11 dc in ring; join with sl st in initial ch 1.
Rnd 2: ch 3 (counts as tr). *ch 5. Skip 1 dc, and tr in 1 dc. Repeat from * 4 times. ch 5. Join with sl st in 3rd ch of initial ch 3.
Rnd 3: sl st in ch 5 space. ch 3 (counts as tr). 6 tr in same ch 5 space. *ch 1. 7 tr in next ch 5 space. Repeat from * 4 times. ch 1. Join with sl st in 3rd ch of initial ch 3.
Rnd 4: ch 1 (counts as dc). dc in 2 tr. *[dc, ch 6, dc] in next tr. dc in 3 tr. ch 1.** dc in 3 tr. Repeat from * 4 times, and from * to ** once more. Join with sl st in initial ch 1. Finish off; weave in ends.

20 NOR'EASTER II
See page 25 in the showcase

The Nor'easter series continues with Nor'easter II, whose trim of chains and loops creates a lacy edge.

Finished diameter: 67mm (2⅝in)
Thread required: 5.5m (6yd)

Foundation ring: ch 6; join with sl st in first ch.
Rnd 1: ch 1 (counts as dc). 11 dc in ring; join with sl st in initial ch 1.
Rnd 2: ch 3 (counts as tr). *ch 5. Skip 1 dc, and tr in 1 dc. Repeat from * 4 times. ch 5. Join with sl st in 3rd ch of initial ch 3.
Rnd 3: sl st in ch 5 space. ch 3 (counts as tr). 6 tr in same ch 5 space. *ch 1. 7 tr in next ch 5 space. Repeat from * 4 times. ch 1. Join with sl st in 3rd ch of initial ch 3.
Rnd 4: sl st in 3 tr. ch 1 (counts as dc). ch 8, and sl st in 8th ch from hook to form loop. dc in the last tr worked in *ch 4. Skip 3 tr, and dc in next ch 1 space. ch 4.** Skip 3 tr, and dc in 1 tr. ch 8, and sl st in 8th ch from hook to form loop. dc in the same tr as last dc. Repeat from * 4 times, and from * to ** once more. Join with sl st in initial ch 1. Finish off; weave in ends.

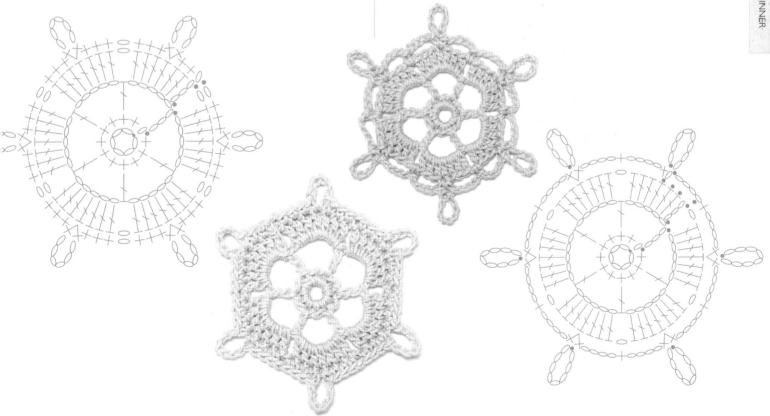

21 NOR'EASTER III
See page 24 in the showcase

The feathery outer edge of Nor'easter III features a chain pattern, overstitched with double and treble crochets.

Finished diameter: 64mm (2½in)
Thread required: 7.3m (8yd)

Foundation ring: ch 6; join with sl st in first ch.
Rnd 1: ch 1 (counts as dc). 11 dc in ring; join with sl st in initial ch 1.
Rnd 2: ch 3 (counts as tr). *ch 5. Skip 1 dc, and tr in 1 dc. Repeat from * 4 times. ch 5. Join with sl st in 3rd ch of initial ch 3.
Rnd 3: sl st in ch 5 space. ch 3 (counts as tr). 6 tr in same ch 5 space. *ch 1. 7 tr in next ch 5 space. Repeat from * 4 times. ch 1. Join with sl st in 3rd ch of initial ch 3.
Rnd 4: ch 1 (counts as dc). *ch 4. Skip 2 tr, and dc in 1 tr. ch 4. Skip 2 tr, and dc in 1 tr. ch 2.** dc in next tr. Repeat from * 4 times, and from * to ** once more. Join with sl st in initial ch 1.
Rnd 5: sl st in next ch 4 space. ch 1 (counts as dc). 4 dc in same ch 4 space. *5 dc in next ch 4 space. [2 tr, ch 2, 2 tr] in next ch 2 space.** 5 dc in next ch 4 space. Repeat from * 4 times, and from * to ** once more. Join with sl st in initial ch 1. Finish off; weave in ends.

22 NOR'EASTER IV
See page 25 in the showcase

In the final design of the Nor'easter series, another layer of chains and trebles is added, to create a large hexagonal snowflake.

Finished diameter: 79mm (3⅛in)
Thread required: 10.1m (11yd)

Foundation ring: ch 6; join with sl st in first ch.
Rnd 1: ch 1 (counts as dc). 11 dc in ring; join with sl st in initial ch 1.
Rnd 2: ch 3 (counts as tr). *ch 5. Skip 1 dc, and tr in 1 dc. Repeat from * 4 times. ch 5. Join with sl st in 3rd ch of initial ch 3.
Rnd 3: sl st in ch 5 space. ch 3 (counts as tr). 6 tr in same ch 5 space. *ch 1. 7 tr in next ch 5 space. Repeat from * 4 times. ch 1. Join with sl st in 3rd ch of initial ch 3.
Rnd 4: sl st in 3 tr. ch 3 (counts as tr). *ch 5. Skip 3 tr, and tr in next ch 1 space. ch 5.** Skip 3 tr, and tr in 1 tr. Repeat from * 4 times, and from * to ** once more. Join with sl st in 3rd ch of initial ch 3.
Rnd 5: sl st in ch 5 space. ch 3 (counts as tr). 5 tr in same ch 5 space. *tr in tr. 6 tr in next ch 5 space.** [tr, ch 2, tr] in tr. 6 tr in next ch 5 space. Repeat from * 4 times, and from * to ** once more. [tr, ch 2, tr] in sl st (the stitch that joined Rnd 4). Join with sl st in 3rd ch of initial ch 3. Finish off; weave in ends.

23 FIRN
See page 24 in the showcase

This dense little snowflake is named after firn, which is old snow that has become granular and compacted.

Finished diameter: 67mm (2⅝in)
Thread required: 7.3m (8yd)

Foundation ring: ch 6; join with sl st in first ch.
Rnd 1: ch 1 (counts as dc). 11 dc in ring; join with sl st in initial ch 1.
Rnd 2: ch 3 (counts as tr). tr in 1 dc. *ch 3. tr in 2 dc. Repeat from * 4 times. ch 3. Join with sl st in 3rd ch of initial ch 3.
Rnd 3: ch 3 (counts as tr). tr in tr. *[2 tr, ch 2, 2 tr] in ch 3 space.** tr in 2 tr. Repeat from * 4 times, and from * to ** once more. Join with sl st in 3rd ch of initial ch 3.
Rnd 4: sl st in 2 tr. ch 1 (counts as dc). dc in tr. *[dc, ch 3, dc] in ch 2 point. dc in 2 tr. ch 2.** Skip 2 tr, and dc in 2 tr. Repeat from * 4 times, and from * to ** once more. Join with sl st in initial ch 1.
Rnd 5: ch 1 (counts as dc). dc in 2 dc. *[2dc, ch 4, 2 dc] in ch 3 space. dc in 3 dc. 2 dc in ch 2 space.** dc in 3 dc. Repeat from * 4 times, and from * to ** once more. Join with sl st in initial ch 1. Finish off; weave in ends.

24 KAAVIE
See page 25 in the showcase

This decorative flake might float down with many others during a Kaavie, a Scottish term for a heavy snowfall.

Finished diameter: 76mm (3in)
Thread required: 7.3m (8yd)

Foundation ring: ch 6; join with sl st in first ch.
Rnd 1: ch 1 (counts as dc). 11 dc in ring; join with sl st in initial ch 1.
Rnd 2: ch 3 (counts as tr). tr in 1 dc. *ch 3. tr in 2 dc. Repeat from * 4 times. ch 3. Join with sl st in 3rd ch of initial ch 3.
Rnd 3: ch 3 (counts as tr). tr in 1 tr. *ch 5. Skip ch 3 space; tr in 2 tr. Repeat from * 4 times. ch 5. Join with sl st in 3rd ch of initial ch 3.
Rnd 4: ch 3 (counts as tr). tr in tr. *[3 tr, ch 2, 3 tr] in ch 5 space.** tr in 2 tr. Repeat from * 4 times, and from * to ** once more. Join with sl st in 3rd ch of initial ch 3.
Rnd 5: ch 1 (counts as dc). *ch 4. dc in next tr. ch 4. [dc, ch 8, dc] in next ch 3 point. ch 4.** Skip 3 tr, and dc in 1 tr. Repeat from * 4 times, and from * to ** once more. Join with sl st in initial ch 1. Finish off; weave in ends.

SKILL LEVEL BEGINNER

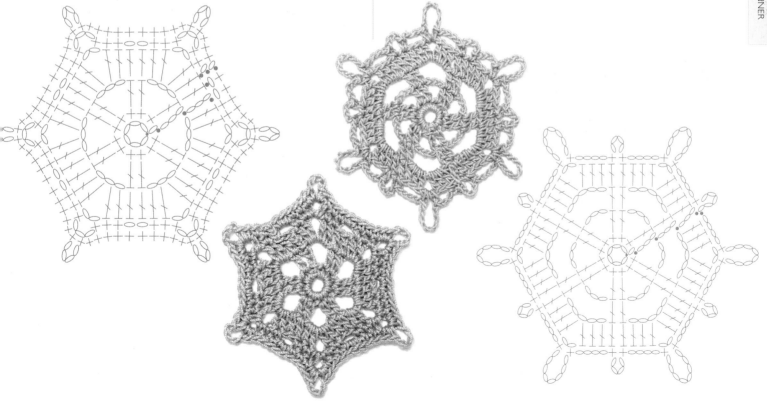

25 ICE PRISM

See page 27 in the showcase

Like an ice prism, this design is characterised by its simple and well-defined shape.

Finished diameter: 67mm (2⅝in)
Thread required: 7.3m (8yd)

Foundation ring: ch 6; join with sl st in first ch.
Rnd 1: ch 1 (counts as dc). 11 dc in ring; join with sl st in initial ch 1.
Rnd 2: ch 3 (counts as tr). tr in 1 dc. *ch 3. tr in 2 dc. Repeat from * 4 times. ch 3. Join with sl st in 3rd ch of initial ch 3.
Rnd 3: ch 1 (counts as dc). dc in tr. *[2 dc, ch 2, 2 dc] in ch 3 point.** dc in 2 tr. Repeat from * 4 times, and from * to ** once more. Join with sl st in initial ch 1.
Rnd 4: ch 3 (counts as tr). tr in 1 dc. *ch 2. [2 tr, ch 2, 2 tr] in next ch 2 point. ch 2.** Skip 2 dc, and tr in 2 dc. Repeat from * 4 times, and from * to ** once more. Join with sl st in 3rd ch of initial ch 3.
Rnd 5: ch 1 (counts as dc). dc in tr. *dc in ch 2 space. dc in 2 tr. [2 dc, ch 4, 2 dc] in ch 2 point. dc in 2 tr. dc in ch 2 space.** dc in 2 tr. Repeat from * 4 times, and from * to ** once more. Join with sl st in initial ch 1. Finish off; weave in ends.

26 AUVERGNASSE

See page 26 in the showcase

A cold northwest wind in central France shares its name with this wispy and elegant crystal.

Finished diameter: 83mm (3¼in)
Thread required: 6.4m (7yd)

Foundation ring: ch 6; join with sl st in first ch.
Rnd 1: ch 1 (counts as first dc). 11 dc in ring; join with sl st in initial ch 1.
Rnd 2: ch 3 (counts as tr). tr in 1 dc. *ch 5. tr in 2 dc. Repeat from * 4 times. ch 5. Join with sl st in 3rd ch of initial ch 3.
Rnd 3: ch 1 (counts as dc). *ch 2. dc in next tr. [3 dc, ch 2, 3 dc] in ch 5 space.** dc in 1 tr. Repeat from * 4 times, and from * to ** once more. Join with sl st in initial ch 1.
Rnd 4: sl st in next ch 2 space. ch 1 (counts as dc). *ch 4. Skip 4 dc, and tr in next ch 2 point. ch 7, and sl st in 6th ch from hook to form loop. ch 8, and sl st in 8th ch from hook. ch 6, and sl st in 6th ch from hook. sl st in 1st ch of ch 7. tr in same point as last tr. ch 4.** Skip 4 dc, and dc in next ch 2 space. Repeat from * 4 times, and from * to ** once more. Join with sl st in initial ch 1. Finish off; weave in ends.

27 FIRNSPIEGEL
See page 26 in the showcase

'Firnspiegel' is a term for the icy glaze that forms when snow melts and refreezes.

Finished diameter: 67mm (2⅝in)
Thread required: 6.4m (7yd)

Foundation ring: ch 6; join with sl st in first ch.
Rnd 1: ch 1 (counts as first dc). 11 dc in ring; join with sl st in initial ch 1.
Rnd 2: ch 1 (counts as dc). dc in 1 dc. *ch 3. dc in 2 dc. Repeat from * 4 times. ch 3. Join with sl st in initial ch 1.
Rnd 3: sl st in dc, and in ch 3 point. ch 3 (counts as tr). ch 2; tr in same ch 3 point. *ch 4. [tr, ch 2, tr] in next ch 3 point. Repeat from * 4 times. ch 4. Join with sl st in 3rd ch of initial ch 3.
Rnd 4: sl st in ch 2 space. ch 1 (counts as dc). ch 3. dc in same ch 2 space. *5 dc in ch 4 space.** [dc, ch 3, dc] in next ch 2 space. Repeat from * 4 times, and from * to ** once more. Join with sl st in initial ch 1.
Rnd 5: sl st in ch 3 point. ch 3 (counts as tr). tr in same ch 3 point. ch 4. 2 tr in same ch 3 point. *Skip 1 dc, and tr in 2 dc. ch 1. Skip 1 dc, and tr in 2 dc.** Skip 1 dc. [2 tr, ch 4, 2 tr] in ch 3 point. Repeat from * 4 times, and from * to ** once more. Join with sl st in 3rd ch of initial ch 3. Finish off; weave in ends.

SKILL LEVEL BEGINNER

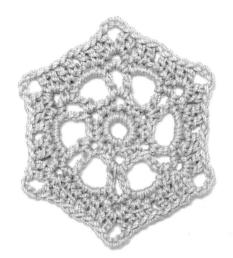
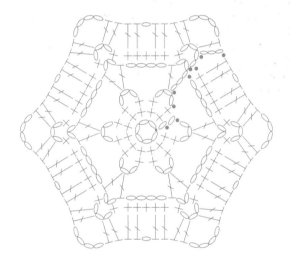

28 NORTE
See page 26 in the showcase

This delicate snowflake is named after the winter north wind in Spain.

Finished diameter: 70mm (2¾in)
Thread required: 5.5m (6yd)

Foundation ring: ch 6; join with sl st in first ch.
Rnd 1: ch 3 (counts as tr). *ch 2. tr in ring. Repeat from * 10 times. ch 2. Join with sl st in 3rd ch of initial ch 3.
Rnd 2: sl st in ch 2 space, and ch 1 (counts as dc). *ch 3. dc in next ch 2 space. Repeat from * 10 times. ch 3. Join with sl st in initial ch 1.
Rnd 3: sl st in ch 3 space, and ch 1 (counts as dc). dc in same ch 3 space. *ch 9, and sl st in 4th ch from hook to form picot. ch 4. sl st in 1st ch of ch 9. 2 dc in same ch 3 space as last dc. [dc, tr] in next ch 3 space. ch 4 and sl st in 4th ch from hook to form picot. [tr, dc] in same ch 3 space.** 2 dc in next ch 3 space. Repeat from * 4 times, and from * to ** once more. Join with sl st in initial ch 1. Finish off; weave in ends.

29 ICE CRYSTAL I
See page 26 in the showcase

This light and lacy flake, the first of the Ice Crystal series, is composed of a simple sequence of chains, slip stitches and double crochets.

Finished diameter: 57mm (2¼in)
Thread required: 5.5m (6yd)

Foundation ring: ch 6; join with sl st in first ch.
Rnd 1: ch 1 (counts as dc). 11 dc in ring; join with sl st in initial ch 1.
Rnd 2: ch 1 (counts as dc). dc in 1 dc. *ch 3. dc in 2 dc. Repeat from * 4 times. ch 3. Join with sl st in initial ch 1.
Rnd 3: sl st in 1 dc, and in ch 3 space. ch 1 (counts as dc). 2 dc in same ch 3 space. *ch 4. 3 dc in next ch 3 space. Repeat from * 4 times. ch 4. Join with sl st in initial ch 1.
Rnd 4: ch 1 (counts as dc). dc in 2 dc. *[2 dc, ch 4, 2 dc] in ch 4 space.** dc in 3 dc. Repeat from * 4 times, and from * to ** once more. Join with sl st in initial ch 1.
Rnd 5: sl st in 1 dc. ch 1 (counts as dc). *ch 3. [3 dc, ch 3, 3 dc] in next ch 4 point. ch 3.** Skip 3 dc, and dc in 1 dc (halfway between points). Repeat from * 4 times, and from * to ** once more. Join with sl st in initial ch 1. Finish off; weave in ends.

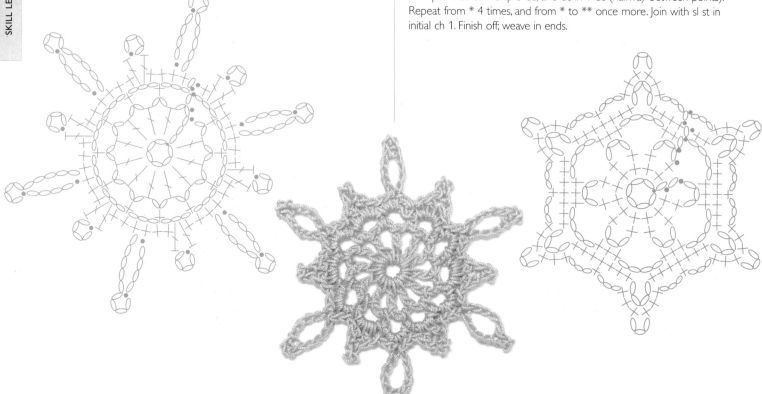

30 ICE CRYSTAL II
See page 26 in the showcase

The second of the Ice Crystal snowflakes is very similar to the first in its construction, but just as with the snowflakes found in nature, a few small changes have created an entirely new appearance.

Finished diameter: 70mm (2¾in)
Thread required: 6.4m (7yd)

Foundation ring: ch 6; join with sl st in first ch.
Rnd 1: ch 1 (counts as dc). 11 dc in ring; join with sl st in initial ch 1.
Rnd 2: ch 1 (counts as dc). dc in 1 dc. *ch 3. dc in 2 dc. Repeat from * 4 times. ch 3. Join with sl st in initial ch 1.
Rnd 3: sl st in 1 dc, and in ch 3 space. ch 1 (counts as dc). 2 dc in same ch 3 space. *ch 4. 3 dc in next ch 3 space. Repeat from * 4 times. ch 4. Join with sl st in initial ch 1.
Rnd 4: ch 1 (counts as dc). dc in 2 dc. *[2 dc, ch 4, 2 dc] in ch 4 space.** dc in 3 dc. Repeat from * 4 times, and from * to ** once more. Join with sl st in initial ch 1.
Rnd 5: ch 1 (counts as dc). *ch 3. Skip 1 dc, and dc in 1 dc. ch 2. Skip 2 dc. [dc, ch 4, dc] in next ch 4 point. ch 8, and sl st in 8th ch from hook to form loop. [dc, ch 4, dc] in same ch 4 point. ch 2.** Skip 2 dc, and dc in 1 dc. Repeat from * 4 times, and from * to ** once more. Join with sl st in initial ch 1. Finish off; weave in ends.

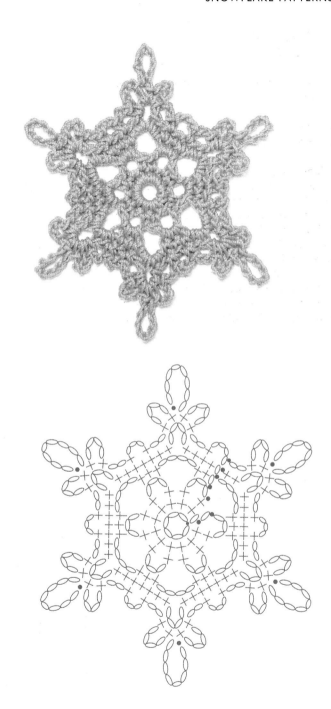

31 SQUALL
See page 26 in the showcase

This snowflake's simple, curved lines suggest calligraphy, embellishing a stormy day.

Finished diameter: 73mm (2⅞in)
Thread required: 7.3m (8yd)

Foundation ring: ch 6; join with sl st in first ch.
Rnd 1: ch 1 (counts as dc). 11 dc in ring; join with sl st in initial ch 1.
Rnd 2: ch 1 (counts as dc). *ch 7. Skip 1 dc and dc in next dc. Repeat from * 4 times. ch 7. Join with sl st in initial ch 1.
Rnd 3: *[5 dc, ch 2, 5 dc] in ch 7 space.** sl st in dc. Repeat from * 4 times, and from * to ** once more. Join with sl st in sl st.
Rnd 4: sl st in 5 dc, and in ch 2 point. ch 1 (counts as dc). ch 8, and dc in same ch 2 point to form loop. *ch 7. [dc, ch 8, dc] in next ch 2 point. Repeat from * 4 times. ch 7. Join with sl st in initial ch 1.
Rnd 5: sl st in ch 8 loop. ch 1 (counts as dc). 4 dc in same ch 8 loop. ch 2. 5 dc in same loop. *8 dc in next ch 7 space.** [5dc, ch 2, 5dc] in next ch 8 loop. Repeat from * 4 times, and from * to ** once more. Join with sl st in initial ch 1. Finish off; weave in ends.

32 FROST MIST
See page 27 in the showcase

Petite and lovely, Frost Mist is the first snowflake in this collection to use the half treble.

Finished diameter: 51mm (2in)
Thread required: 4.6m (5yd)

Foundation ring: ch 6; join with sl st in first ch.
Rnd 1: ch 1 (counts as first dc). 11 dc in ring; join with sl st in initial ch 1.
Rnd 2: ch 3 (counts as tr). tr in 1 dc. *ch 5. tr in 2 dc. Repeat from * 4 times. ch 5. Join with sl st in 3rd ch of initial ch 3.
Rnd 3: ch 1 (counts as dc). *ch 4, and sl st in 4th ch from hook to form picot. dc in next tr. [dc, htr, tr, ch 4, tr, htr, dc] in next ch 5 space.** dc in 1 tr. Repeat from * 4 times, and from * to ** once more. Join with sl st in initial ch 1. Finish off; weave in ends.

33 CAVABURD
See page 27 in the showcase

This soft, rounded design takes its name from a Shetland Island term for a thick snowfall.

Finished diameter: 60mm (2⅜in)
Thread required: 6.4m (7yd)

Foundation ring: ch 6; join with sl st in first ch.
Rnd 1: ch 3 (counts as tr). 1 tr in ring. *ch 2. 2 tr in ring. Repeat from * 4 times. ch 2. Join with sl st in 3rd ch of initial ch 3.
Rnd 2: ch 3 (counts as tr). tr in tr. *[tr, ch 2, tr] in ch 2 space.** tr in 2 tr. Repeat from * 4 times, and from * to ** once more. Join with sl st in 3rd ch of initial ch 3.
Rnd 3: ch 1 (counts as dc). dc in 1 tr. *ch 3. [dc, ch 8, dc] in next ch 2 space. ch 3.** Skip 1 tr, and dc in 2 tr. Repeat from * 4 times, and from * to ** once more. Join with sl st in initial ch 1.
Rnd 4: sl st in dc, and in ch 3 space. ch 1 (counts as dc). 2 dc in same ch 3 space. *6 dc in ch 8 loop.** 3 dc in each of the next 2 ch 3 spaces (skipping the 2 dc between them). Repeat from * 4 times, and from * to ** once more. 3 dc in next ch 3 space. Join with sl st in initial ch 1. Finish off; weave in ends.

34 NORTHER
See page 27 in the showcase

This flower-shaped flake might be found swirling in a norther, or cold, northerly wind.

Finished diameter: 54mm (2⅛in)
Thread required: 6.4m (7yd)

Foundation ring: ch 6; join with sl st in first ch.
Rnd 1: ch 3 (counts as first tr). 11 tr in ring; join with sl st in 3rd ch of ch 3.
Rnd 2: ch 1 (counts as first dc). *[dc, ch 8, dc] in next tr to form loop.** dc in 1 tr. Repeat from * 4 times, and from * to ** once more. Join with sl st in initial ch 1.
Rnd 3: *sl st in next dc. In the next ch 8 loop, work the following sequence of stitches: [3 dc, htr, tr, ch 1, tr, htr, 3 dc]. sl st in next dc; ch 2. Skip 1 dc. Repeat from * 5 times; join with sl st in the sl st at the beginning of the first loop.
Rnd 4: sl st in 2 dc. ch 1 (counts as dc). dc in dc. *dc in htr, and in tr. [dc, ch 2, dc] in ch 1 space. dc in tr, in htr, and in 2 dc.** Skip dc, skip sl st, and skip ch 2 space. Then skip sl st, and skip 1 dc (the first dc in the next loop). dc in 2 dc. Repeat from ** 4 times, and from * to ** once more. Join with sl st in initial ch 1. Finish off; weave in ends.

35 HALO
See page 27 in the showcase

This snowflake's shape is reminiscent of a halo, the ring that appears when light is scattered by ice crystals in the air.

Finished diameter: 57mm (2¼in)
Thread required: 7.3m (8yd)

Foundation ring: ch 6; join with sl st in first ch.
Rnd 1: ch 1 (counts as first dc). 11 dc in ring; join with sl st in initial ch 1.
Rnd 2: ch 1 (counts as first dc). *[dc, ch 6, dc] in 1 dc.** dc in 1 dc. Repeat from * 4 times, and from * to ** once more. Join with sl st in initial ch 1.
Rnd 3: ch 1 (counts as dc). *[4 dc, ch 2, 4 dc] in next ch 6 loop.** Skip 1 dc (at the bottom of the loop). dc in 1 dc (halfway between loops). Repeat from *4 times, and from * to ** once more. Join with sl st in initial ch 1.
Rnd 4: sl st in 4 dc, and in ch 2 point. ch 1 (counts as dc). *ch 4. Skip 4 dc, and tr in 1 dc (halfway between petals). ch 4.** dc in next ch 2 point. Repeat from * 4 times, and from * to ** once more. Join with sl st in initial ch 1.
Rnd 5: sl st in ch 4 space, and ch 3 (counts as first tr). 3 tr in the same ch 4 space *4 tr in next ch 4 space.** [tr, ch 2, tr] in dc. 4 tr in next ch 4 space. Repeat from * 4 times, and from * to ** once more. [tr, ch 2, tr] in sl st (the stitch that joined Rnd 4). Join with sl st in 3rd ch of initial ch 3. Finish off; weave in ends.

36 BORA
See page 27 in the showcase

This design, which serves to introduce the double treble crochet, takes its name from a very cold downhill wind.

Finished diameter: 67mm (2⅝in)
Thread required: 5.5m (6yd)

Foundation ring: ch 6; join with sl st in first ch.
Rnd 1: ch 5 (counts as dtr). *ch 1. 1 dtr in ring. Repeat from * 10 times. ch 1. Join with sl st in 5th ch of ch 5.
Rnd 2: ch 3 (counts as tr). *2 tr in ch 1 space. tr in dtr. [tr, ch 2, tr] in next ch 1 space.** tr in dtr. Repeat from * 4 times, and from * to ** once more. Join with sl st in 3rd ch of ch 3
Rnd 3: sl st in tr, and ch 1 (counts as dc). *ch 4. dc in next tr. ch 2. Skip 2 tr, and tr in ch 2 point. ch 6, and sl st in 6th ch from hook to form loop. tr in same ch 2 point. ch 2.** Skip 2 tr, and dc in 1 tr. Repeat from * 4 times, and from * to ** once more. Join with sl st in initial ch 1. Finish off; weave in ends.

37 NIEVE PENITENTE
See page 28 in the showcase

Nieve penitente (also called penitent ice) is a pillar of compacted snow or ice, found most often in the Chilean Andes.

Finished diameter: 67mm (2⅝in)
Thread required: 4.6m (5yd)

Foundation ring: ch 4; join with sl st in first ch.
Rnd 1: ch 5 (counts as dtr). *ch 4. dtr in ring. Repeat from * 4 times. ch 4. Join with sl st in 5th ch of initial ch 5.
Rnd 2: ch 1 (counts as dc). *[3 dc, ch 2, 3 dc] in next ch 4 space.** dc in dtr. Repeat from * 4 times, and from * to ** once more. Join with sl st in initial ch 1.
Rnd 3: ch 1 (counts as dc). ch 8, and sl st in 4th ch from hook to form picot. ch 4. dc in same stitch as initial sl st (the stitch that joined Rnd 2). *ch 2. [dc, ch 4, dc] in next ch 2 point. ch 2.** Skip 3 dc, and dc in 1 dc. ch 8, and sl st in 4th ch from hook to form picot. ch 4. dc in same dc as last dc. Repeat from * 4 times, and from * to ** once more. Join with sl st in initial ch 1. Finish off; weave in ends.

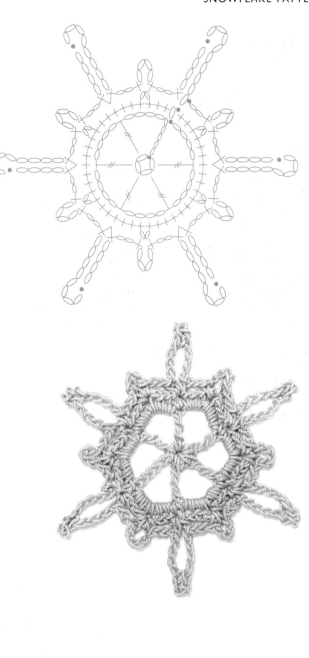

SKILL LEVEL INTERMEDIATE

38 THUNDERSNOW
See page 28 in the showcase

This pretty, compact snowflake might have fallen in a rare winter thunderstorm.

Finished diameter: 70mm (2¾in)
Thread required: 7.3m (8yd)

Foundation ring: ch 6; join with sl st in first ch.
Rnd 1: ch 1 (counts as first dc). 11 dc in ring; join with sl st in initial ch 1.
Rnd 2: ch 5 (counts as dtr). *ch 2. dtr in next dc. Repeat from * 10 times. ch 2. Join with sl st in 5th ch of initial ch 5.
Rnd 3: sl st in ch 2 space. ch 1 (counts as dc). 2 dc in same ch 2 space. *[2 dc, ch 2, 2 dc] in next ch 2 space.** 3 dc in next ch 2 space. Repeat from * 4 times, and from * to ** once more. Join with sl st in initial ch 1.
Rnd 4: ch 1 (counts as dc). *ch 2. Skip 1 dc, and dc in 3 dc. [dc, ch 4, dc] in ch 2 point.** dc in 3 dc. Repeat from * 4 times, and from * to ** once more. dc in 2 dc. Join with sl st in initial ch 1.
Rnd 5: sl st in ch 2 space, and ch 1 (counts as dc). dc in same space. *Skip 1 dc, and dc in 2 dc. Skip 1 dc. [2 dc, ch 4, 2, dc] in ch 4 point. Skip 1 dc, and dc in 2 dc.** Skip 1 dc. 2 dc in ch 2 space. Repeat from * 4 times, and from * to ** once more. Join with sl st in initial ch 1. Finish off; weave in ends.

39 KAIKIAS
See page 28 in the showcase

This smooth-edged design takes its name from the Greek word for the cold northeast wind.

Finished diameter: 60mm (2⅜in)
Thread required: 6.4m (7yd)

Foundation ring: ch 6; join with sl st in first ch.
Rnd 1: ch 1 (counts as first dc). 11 dc in ring; join with sl st in initial ch 1.
Rnd 2: ch 3 (counts as tr). *ch 2. dtr in 1 dc. ch 2.** tr in 1 dc. Repeat from * 4 times, and from * to ** once more. Join with sl st in 3rd ch of initial ch 3.
Rnd 3: sl st in next ch 2 space. ch 1 (counts as dc). htr and tr in same ch 2 space. *[tr, ch 2, tr] in dtr. [tr, htr, dc] in ch 2 space.** [dc, htr, tr] in next ch 2 space. Repeat from * 4 times, and from * to ** once more. Join with sl st in initial ch 1.
Rnd 4: *ch 3. Skip htr. htr in 2 tr. [htr, ch 3, htr] in ch 2 point. htr in 2 tr. ch 3.** Skip htr. sl st in 2 dc. Repeat from * 4 times, and from * to ** once more. Skip htr, and join with sl st in dc. Finish off; weave in ends.

40 SILVER FROST
See page 29 in the showcase

Rounded and encircled, this snowflake is named after the icy glaze formed on exposed objects during an ice storm.

Finished diameter: 70mm (2¾in)
Thread required: 8.2m (9yd)

Foundation ring: ch 6; join with sl st in first ch.
Rnd 1: ch 1 (counts as dc). 11 dc in ring; join with sl st in initial ch 1.
Rnd 2: ch 1 (counts as dc). *[dc, ch 8, dc] in 1 dc.** dc in 1 dc. Repeat from * 4 times, and from * to ** once more. Join with sl st in initial ch 1.
Rnd 3: *sl st in next dc (at the beginning of the next loop). Work the following sequence of stitches in the ch 8 loop: [3 dc, htr, tr, ch 1, tr, htr, 3 dc]. sl st in 1 dc (at the end of the loop). ch 1. skip 1 dc. Repeat from * 5 times; join with sl st in sl st.
Rnd 4: sl st in 3 dc, in htr, in tr, and in the ch 1 space at the top of the loop. ch 1 (counts as dc). ch 6. dc in the same ch 1 space. *ch 8. [dc, ch 6, dc] in the ch 1 space at the top of the next loop. Repeat from * 4 times. ch 8. join with sl st in initial ch 1.
Rnd 5: *[3 dc, htr, 3 dc] in ch 6 loop. sl st in the next dc (at the end of the loop). 9 dc in ch 8 space.** sl st in next dc (at the beginning of the next loop). Repeat from * 4 times, and from * to ** once more. Join with sl st in sl st. Finish off; weave in ends.

41 ALBERTA CLIPPER
See page 29 in the showcase

This star-shaped snowflake might be dropped by an Alberta Clipper, a low-pressure system originating near Alberta, Canada.

Finished diameter: 79mm (3⅛in)
Thread required: 5.5m (6yd)

Foundation ring: ch 6; join with sl st in first ch.
Rnd 1: ch 3 (counts as tr). 1 tr in ring. *ch 2. 2 tr in ring. Repeat from * 4 times. ch 2. Join with sl st in 3rd ch of initial ch 3.
Rnd 2: ch 1 (counts as dc). *ch 2. dc in next tr. [dc, ch 3, dc] in ch 2 space.** dc in 1 tr. Repeat from * 4 times, and from * to ** once more. Join with sl st in initial ch 1.
Rnd 3: sl st in ch 2 point, and ch 1 (counts as dc). ch 4. dc in same ch 2 point. *ch 1. dc in next ch 3 point. ch 7, and sl st in 4th ch from hook to form picot. ch 8, and sl st in 8th ch from hook. ch 4, and sl st in 4th ch from hook. dc in 3rd and 2nd ch of ch 7. ch 1. 1 dc in the last ch 3 point worked in ch 1.** [dc, ch 4, dc] in next ch 2 point. Repeat from * 4 times, and from * to ** once more. Join with sl st in initial ch 1. Finish off; weave in ends.

42 TAKU
See page 28 in the showcase

The Taku wind is a gusty east-northeast wind that blows during the winter in Alaska, and may reach hurricane force.

Finished diameter: 95mm (3¾in)
Thread required: 6.4m (7yd)

Foundation ring: ch 6; join with sl st in first ch.
Rnd 1: ch 1 (counts as first dc). 11 dc in ring; join with sl st in initial ch 1.
Rnd 2: ch 5 (counts as dtr). *ch 2. dtr in next dc. Repeat from * 10 times. ch 2. Join with sl st in 5th ch of initial ch 5.
Rnd 3: sl st in ch 2 space. ch 1 (counts as dc). 2 dc in same ch 2 space. *[2 dc, ch 2, 2 dc] in next ch 2 space.** 3 dc in next ch 2 space. Repeat from * 4 times, and from * to ** once more. Join with sl st in initial ch 1.
Rnd 4: sl st in 1 dc. ch 1 (counts as dc). *ch 4. tr in next ch 2 point. ch 7, and sl st in 6th ch from hook to form picot. ch 8, and sl st in 4th ch from hook. ch 3, and sl st in 1st ch of ch 8. ch 6, and sl st in 6th ch from hook. sl st in 1st ch of ch 7. tr in same ch 2 point as last tr. ch 4.** Skip 3 dc, and dc in 1 dc (halfway between points). Repeat from * 4 times, and from * to ** once more. Join with sl st in initial ch 1. Finish off; weave in ends.

43 | ALPINE GLACIER
See page 29 in the showcase

This beautiful snowflake would be at home on an alpine glacier, high in the mountains.

Finished diameter: 73mm (2⅞in)
Thread required: 5.5m (6yd)

Foundation ring: ch 6; join with sl st in first ch.
Rnd 1: ch 1 (counts as dc). 11 dc in ring; join with sl st in initial ch 1.
Rnd 2: ch 1 (counts as dc). *[dc, ch 6, dc] in next dc.** dc in 1 dc. Repeat from * 4 times, and from * to ** once more. Join with sl st in initial ch 1.
Rnd 3: sl st in dc, and in first ch of ch 6 loop. sl st in loop. ch 1 (counts as dc). dc in loop. ch 2. 2 dc in same loop. *ch 3. [2 dc, ch 2, 2 dc] in next ch 6 loop. Repeat from * 4 times. ch 3. Join with sl st in initial ch 1.
Rnd 4: sl st in dc, and in ch 2 point. ch 1 (counts as dc). *ch 5, and sl st in 4th ch from hook to form picot. ch 8, and sl st in 8th ch from hook. ch 4, and sl st in 4th ch from hook. sl st in 1st ch of ch 5. dc in same ch 2 point. ch 2. dc in next ch 3 space. ch 4 and sl st in 4th ch from hook. dc in same ch 3 space as last dc. ch 2.** dc in next ch 2 point. Repeat from * 4 times, and from * to ** once more. Join with sl st in initial ch 1. Finish off; weave in ends.

44 BISE NOIR
See page 28 in the showcase

The Bise is a cool wind that usually blows in the spring and brings good weather to parts of France and Switzerland. In the winter, however, it can bring clouds with rain, snow or hail. This Bise is called a Bise Noir, or 'Black Bise'.

Finished diameter: 67mm (2⅝in)
Thread required: 6.4m (7yd)

Foundation ring: ch 6; join with sl st in first ch.
Rnd 1: ch 1 (counts as first dc). 11 dc in ring; join with sl st in initial ch 1.
Rnd 2: ch 5 (counts as dtr). dtr in 1 dc. *ch 4. dtr in 2 dc. Repeat from * 4 times. ch 4. Join with sl st in 5th ch of initial ch 5.
Rnd 3: ch 1 (counts as dc). dc in dtr. *[dc, htr, tr] in ch 4 space. ch 5, and sl st in 5th ch from hook to form loop. [tr, htr, dc] in same ch 4 space.** dc in 2 dtr. Repeat from * 4 times, and from * to ** once more. Join with sl st in initial ch 1.
Rnd 4: ch 1 (counts as dc). *ch 4. dc in 1 dc. ch 3. [2 dc, ch 3, 2 dc] in next ch 5 loop. ch 3.** Skip tr, htr, and 1 dc. dc in 1 dc. Repeat from * 4 times, and from * to ** once more. Join with sl st in initial ch 1. Finish off; weave in ends.

45 AUFEIS I
See page 28 in the showcase

Aufeis is a term for the layered ice that forms in Arctic stream beds – as water emerges on top of the existing ice, it freezes, and another layer forms.

Finished diameter: 64mm (2½in)
Thread required: 6.4m (7yd)

Foundation ring: ch 6; join with sl st in first ch.
Rnd 1: ch 1 (counts as first dc). 11 dc in ring; join with sl st in initial ch 1.
Rnd 2: ch 1 (counts as dc). dc in 1 dc. *ch 5. dc in 2 dc. Repeat from * 4 times. ch 5. Join with sl st in initial ch 1.
Rnd 3: ch 3 (counts as tr). tr in dc. *3 dc in ch 5 point.** tr in 2 dc. Repeat from * 4 times, and from * to ** once more. Join with sl st in 3rd ch of initial ch 3.
Rnd 4: ch 3 (counts as tr). tr in tr. *tr in 1 dc. [tr, ch 2, tr] in 1 dc. tr in 1 dc.** tr in 2 tr. Repeat from * 4 times, and from * to ** once more. Join with sl st in 3rd ch of initial ch 3.
Rnd 5: ch 1 (counts as dc). dc in 3 tr. *[dc, ch 6, dc] in ch 2 point.** dc in 6 tr. Repeat from * 4 times, and from * to ** once more. dc in 2 tr. Join with sl st in initial ch 1. Finish off; weave in ends.

46 AUFEIS II
See page 29 in the showcase

Aufeis II begins with the first four rounds of Aufeis I, and then adds two more thick rounds, to build a larger, but equally solid, snowflake.

Finished diameter: 73mm (2⅞in)
Thread required: 9.1m (10yd)

Foundation ring: ch 6; join with sl st in first ch.
Rnd 1: ch 1 (counts as first dc). 11 dc in ring; join with sl st in initial ch 1.
Rnd 2: ch 1 (counts as dc). dc in 1 dc. *ch 5. dc in 2 dc. Repeat from * 4 times. ch 5. Join with sl st in initial ch 1.
Rnd 3: ch 3 (counts as tr). tr in dc. *3 dc in ch 5 point.** tr in 2 dc. Repeat from * 4 times, and from * to ** once more. Join with sl st in 3rd ch of initial ch 3.
Rnd 4: ch 3 (counts as tr). tr in tr. *tr in 1 dc. [tr, ch 2, tr] in 1 dc. tr in 1 dc.** tr in 2 tr. Repeat from * 4 times, and from * to ** once more. Join with sl st in 3rd ch of initial ch 3.
Rnd 5: ch 1 (counts as dc). *ch 3. dc in next tr. ch 3. [dc, ch 7, dc] in next ch 2 point. ch 3.** Skip 2 tr, and dc in 1 tr. Repeat from * 4 times, and from * to ** once more. Join with sl st in initial ch 1.
Rnd 6: sl st in next ch 3 space. ch 1 (counts as dc). 2 dc in same ch 3 space. *2 tr in next ch 3 space. [3 dc, ch 3, 3 dc] in ch 7 loop. 2 tr in next ch 3 space.** 3 dc in next ch 3 space. Repeat from * 4 times, and from * to ** once more. Join with sl st in initial ch 1. Finish off; weave in ends.

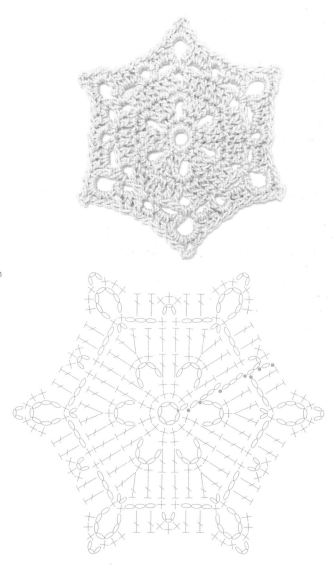

47 SLEET I
See page 29 in the showcase

This crystalline flower is the delicate first snowflake of the Sleet pair.

Finished diameter: 54mm (2⅛in)
Thread required: 5.5m (6yd)

Foundation ring: ch 6; join with sl st in first ch.
Rnd 1: ch 1 (counts as first dc). 11 dc in ring; join with sl st in initial ch 1.
Rnd 2: ch 1 (counts as dc). dc in 1 dc. *ch 5. dc in 2 dc. Repeat from * 4 times. ch 5. Join with sl st in initial ch 1.
Rnd 3: ch 1 (counts as dc). dc in dc. *ch 4. dtr in top of next ch 5 point. ch 4.** dc in 2 dc. Repeat from * 4 times, and from * to ** once more. Join with sl st in initial ch 1.
Rnd 4: sl st in dc. *4 dc in next ch 4 space. [dc, ch 2, dc] in dtr. 4 dc in ch 4 space.** sl st in 2 dc. Repeat from * 4 times, and from * to ** once more. Join with sl st in sl st. Finish off; weave in ends.

48 SLEET II
See page 30 in the showcase

The second design of the Sleet pair begins with the same central flower, which is then surrounded with a strong, hexagonal border.

Finished diameter: 70mm (2¾in)
Thread required: 8.2m (9yd)

Foundation ring: ch 6; join with sl st in first ch.
Rnd 1: ch 1 (counts as first dc). 11 dc in ring; join with sl st in initial ch 1.
Rnd 2: ch 1 (counts as dc). dc in 1 dc. *ch 5. dc in 2 dc. Repeat from * 4 times. ch 5. Join with sl st in initial ch 1.
Rnd 3: ch 1 (counts as dc). dc in dc. *ch 4. dtr in top of next ch 5 point. ch 4.** dc in 2 dc. Repeat from * 4 times, and from * to ** once more. Join with sl st in initial ch 1.
Rnd 4: sl st in dc, and in first 2 ch of next ch 4. sl st in ch 4 space. ch 1 (counts as dc). 2 dc in same ch 4 space. *[dc, ch 4, dc] in dtr. 3 dc in next ch 4 space. ch 2.** 3 dc in next ch 4 space. Repeat from * 4 times, and from * to ** once more. Join with sl st in initial ch 1.
Rnd 5: ch 3 (counts as tr). tr in 2 dc. *Skip next dc, and [2 dc, ch 4, 2 dc] in ch 4 point. Skip 1 dc, and tr in 3 dc. 1 tr in ch 2 space.** tr in 3 dc. Repeat from * 4 times, and from * to ** once more. Join with sl st in 3rd ch of initial ch 3. Finish off; weave in ends.

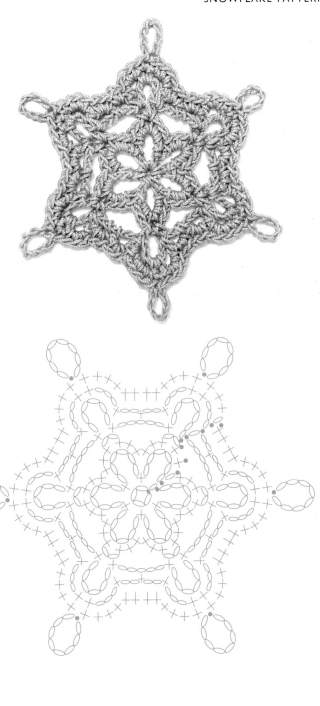

49 VIUGA
See page 30 in the showcase

Composed of layers of loops and single crochets, this snowflake is named after a cold northeast storm in the Russian steppes.

Finished diameter: 76mm (3in)
Thread required: 7.3m (8yd)

Foundation ring: ch 4; join with sl st in first ch.

Rnd 1: ch 1 (counts as dc). *ch 6. dc in ring to form loop. Repeat from * 4 times. ch 6. Join with sl st in initial ch 1.

Rnd 2: sl st in first ch 6 loop. ch 1 (counts as dc). In same ch 6 loop work: [2 dc, ch 2, 3 dc]. [3 dc, ch 2, 3 dc] in each of the 5 remaining loops. Join with sl st in initial ch 1.

Rnd 3: sl st in 2 dc, and in ch 2 point. ch 1 (counts as dc). ch 6, and dc in same ch 2 point. *ch 5. [dc, ch 6, dc] in next ch 2 point. Repeat from * 4 times. ch 5; join with sl st in initial ch 1.

Rnd 4: ch 1 (counts as dc). *ch 3. 2 dc in top of ch 6 loop. ch 3. dc in next dc. ch 2. dc in the middle of the next ch 5 space, and ch 2.** dc in next dc. Repeat from * 4 times, and from * to ** once more. Join with sl st in initial ch 1.

Rnd 5: sl st in ch 3 space, and ch 1 (counts as dc). 2 dc in same space. *dc in 1 dc. ch 8, and sl st in 8th ch from hook to form loop. dc in 1 dc. 3 dc in ch 3 space. 2 dc in each of the next 2 ch 2 spaces.** 3 dc in ch 3 space. Repeat from * 4 times, and once more from * to **. Join with sl st in initial ch 1. Finish off; weave in ends.

SKILL LEVEL INTERMEDIATE

50 SNOW MOON
See page 31 in the showcase

This gorgeous, lace-edged flake might be found sparkling under the Snow Moon, the February full moon.

Finished diameter: 76mm (3in)
Thread required: 7.3m (8yd)

Foundation ring: ch 6; join with sl st in first ch.
Rnd 1: ch 1 (counts as dc). 11 dc in ring; join with sl st in initial ch 1.
Rnd 2: ch 3 (counts as tr). *ch 2. tr in 1 dc. Repeat from * 10 times. ch 2. Join with sl st in 3rd ch of initial ch 3.
Rnd 3: ch 1 (counts as dc). *2 dc in ch 2 space. dc in tr. [dc, ch 2, dc] in next ch 2 space.** dc in tr. Repeat from * 4 times, and from * to ** once more. Join with sl st in initial ch 1.
Rnd 4: ch 3 (counts as tr). *ch 2. Skip 2 dc, and tr in 2 dc. [tr, ch 3, tr] in ch 2 point.** tr in 2 dc. Repeat from * 4 times, and from * to ** once more. tr in 1 dc. Join with sl st in 3rd ch of initial ch 3.
Rnd 5: sl st in ch 2 space, and ch 1 (counts as dc). ch 4. dc in same ch 2 space. *ch 3. [dc, ch 4, dc, ch 8, dc, ch 4, dc] in ch 3 point. ch 3.** [dc, ch 4, dc] in next ch 2 space. Repeat from * 4 times, and from * to ** once more. Join with sl st in initial ch 1. Finish off; weave in ends.

51 NEMERE
See page 31 in the showcase

This stately design might be blown by the Nemere, a stormy fall wind in Hungary.

Finished diameter: 79mm (3⅛in)
Thread required: 8.2m (9yd)

Foundation ring: ch 6; join with sl st in first ch.
Rnd 1: ch 3 (counts as tr). 11 tr in ring; join with sl st in 3rd ch of initial ch 3.
Rnd 2: ch 1 (counts as dc). dc in 1 tr. *ch 4. dc in 2 tr. Repeat from * 4 times. ch 4. Join with sl st in initial ch 1.
Rnd 3: ch 1 (counts as dc). dc in dc. *[2 dc, ch 3, 2 dc] in ch 4 space.** dc in 2 dc. Repeat from * 4 times, and from * to ** once more. Join with sl st in initial ch 1.
Rnd 4: ch 1 (counts as dc). dc in 1 dc. *ch 4. In the next ch 3 point work: [tr; ch 7, and sl st in 7th ch from hook to form loop; tr.] ch 4.** Skip 2 dc, and dc in 2 dc. Repeat from * 4 times, and from * to ** once more. Join with sl st in initial ch 1.
Rnd 5: sl st in dc, and in ch 4 space. ch 1 (counts as dc). 3 dc in same space. *dc in tr. [3 dc, ch 2, 3 dc] in ch 7 loop. dc in next tr.** 4 dc in each of the next 2 ch 4 spaces. Repeat from * 4 times, and from * to ** once more. 4 dc in next ch 4 space. Join with sl st in initial ch 1. Finish off; weave in ends.

52 RIMED CRYSTAL
See page 31 in the showcase

This snowflake's serrated outer edge brings to mind photographs of rimed crystals, snowflakes covered with tiny frozen droplets.

Finished diameter: 64mm (2½in)
Thread required: 7.3m (8yd)

Foundation ring: ch 4; join with sl st in first ch.
Rnd 1: ch 3 (counts as tr). *ch 3. tr in ring. Repeat from * 4 times. ch 3, and join in 3rd ch of initial ch 3.
Rnd 2: sl st in ch 3 space. ch 3 (counts as tr). tr in same space. ch 2; 2 tr in same ch 3 space. [2 tr, ch 2, 2 tr] in each of the 5 remaining ch 3 spaces. Join with sl st in 3rd ch of initial ch 3.
Rnd 3: sl st in tr, and in ch 2 point. ch 3 (counts as tr). 2 tr in same ch 2 point, ch 2, and 3 tr in same point. *ch 2. [3 tr, ch 2, 3 tr] in next ch 2 point. Repeat from * 4 times. ch 2. Join with sl st in 3rd ch of initial ch 3.
Rnd 4: ch 1 (counts as dc). [ch 2, dc] in each of the next 2 tr. ch 2. *[dc, ch 4, dc] in ch 2 point. [ch 2, dc] in each of the next 3 tr. dc in ch 2 space.** [dc, ch 2] in each of the next 3 tr. Repeat from * 4 times, and from * to ** once more. Join with sl st in initial ch 1. Finish off; weave in ends.

SKILL LEVEL INTERMEDIATE

53 DCHARNITZER
See page 30 in the showcase

This swirling pattern is named after a cold north wind in Tyrol, Austria.

Finished diameter: 70mm (2¾in)
Thread required: 5.5m (6yd)

Foundation ring: ch 6; join with sl st in first ch.
Rnd 1: ch 3 (counts as tr). *ch 2. tr in ring. Repeat from * 10 times. ch 2. Join with sl st in 3rd ch of initial ch 3.
Rnd 2: sl st in ch 2 space, and ch 1 (counts as dc). *ch 3. dc in next ch 2 space. Repeat from * 10 times. ch 3. Join with sl st in initial ch 1.
Rnd 3: sl st in ch 3 space, and ch 1 (counts as dc). ch 2. dc in same ch 3 space. *[dc, tr, ch 2, tr, dc] in next ch 3 space.** [dc, ch 2, dc] in next ch 3 space. Repeat from * 4 times, and from * to ** once more. Join with sl st in initial ch 1.
Rnd 4: sl st in ch 2 point, and ch 1 (counts as dc). *ch 3. Skip 2 dc, and skip tr. 2 dc in next ch 2 point. ch 8, and sl st in 8th ch from hook to form loop. 2 dc in same ch 2 point. ch 3.** Skip tr, and skip 2 dc. dc in next ch 2 point. Repeat from * 4 times, and from * to ** once more. Join with sl st in initial ch 1. Finish off; weave in ends.

54 JURAN
See page 31 in the showcase

This little flake might have come in on the Juran, a cold, snowy wind blowing from the Jura Mountains in Switzerland.

Finished diameter: 54mm (2⅛in)
Thread required: 3.7m (4yd)

Foundation ring: ch 6; join with sl st in first ch.
Rnd 1: ch 1 (counts as first dc). 11 dc in ring; join with sl st in initial ch 1.
Rnd 2: ch 1 (counts as first dc), and dc in next dc. *ch 2. dc in next 2 dc. Repeat from * 4 times. ch 2. Join with sl st in initial ch 1.
Rnd 3: ch 1 (counts as dc). dc in dc. *[htr, tr] in ch 2 space. ch 6, and sl st in 6th ch from hook to make picot. ch 8, and sl st in 8th ch from hook. ch 6, and sl st in 6th ch from hook. sl st in top of last tr made. htr in same ch 2 space as last tr.** dc in 2 dc. Repeat from * 4 times, and from * to ** once more. Join with sl st in initial ch 1. Finish off; weave in ends.

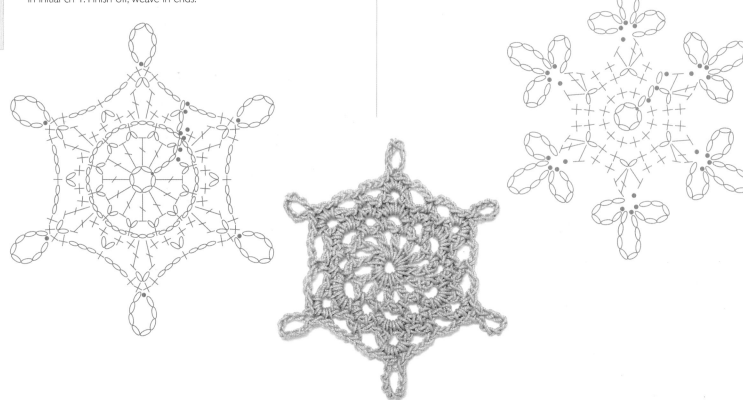

55 ICICLE
See page 30 in the showcase

Close your eyes, and you can picture this graceful flake drifting by a row of icicles, outside the window.

Finished diameter: 89mm (3½in)
Thread required: 6.4m (7yd)

Foundation ring: ch 6; join with sl st in first ch.
Rnd 1: ch 1 (counts as first dc). 11 dc in ring; join with sl st in initial ch 1.
Rnd 2: ch 1 (counts as dc). dc in 1 dc. *ch 5. dc in 2 dc. Repeat from * 4 times. ch 5. Join with sl st in initial ch 1.
Rnd 3: ch 3 (counts as tr). tr in dc. *ch 2. dc in ch 5 point. ch 2.** tr in 2 dc. Repeat from * 4 times, and from * to ** once more. Join with sl st in 3rd ch of initial ch 3.
Rnd 4: sl st in tr, and in ch 2 space. ch 1 (counts as dc). dc in same ch 2 space. *[dc, ch 2, dc] in dc. 2 dc in ch 2 space. ch 2.** Skip 2 tr; 2 dc in next ch 2 space. Repeat from * 4 times, and from * to ** once more. Join with sl st in initial ch 1.
Rnd 5: ch 1 (counts as dc). *ch 4. tr in next ch 2 point. ch 8, and sl st in 4th ch from hook to form picot. ch 4. sl st in top of last tr made. ch 4. Skip 2 dc, and dc in 1 dc. [dc, ch 4, dc] in ch 2 space.** dc in 1 dc. Repeat from * 4 times, and from * to ** once more. Join with sl st in initial ch 1. Finish off; weave in ends.

56 BURGA
See page 31 in the showcase

This airy flower of a snowflake could have fallen during a Burga, a northeast snowstorm in Alaska.

Finished diameter: 70mm (2¾in)
Thread required: 8.2m (9yd)

Foundation ring: ch 6; join with sl st in first ch.
Rnd 1: ch 1 (counts as dc). 11 dc in ring; join with sl st in initial ch 1.
Rnd 2: ch 3 (counts as tr). *ch 2, and tr in next dc. Repeat from * 10 times. ch 2. Join with sl st in 3rd ch of initial ch 3.
Rnd 3: sl st in next ch 2 space; ch 1 (counts as dc). dc in same ch 2 space. * ch 2. 2 dc in next ch 2 space. Repeat from * 10 times. ch 2. Join with sl st in initial ch 1.
Rnd 4: sl st in dc, and in ch 2 space. ch 1 (counts as dc). *ch 3. Skip 2 dc; 2 tr in next ch 2 space. ch 3.** Skip 2 dc; 1 dc in next ch 2 space. Repeat from * 4 times, and from * to ** once more. Join with sl st in initial ch 1.
Rnd 5: *ch 5. tr in next 2 tr. ch 5.** sl st in next dc (halfway between points). Repeat from * 4 times, and from * to ** once more. Join with sl st in sl st.
Rnd 6: *5dc in ch 5 space. [dc, tr] in tr. ch 2. [tr, dc] in next tr. 5 dc in ch 5 space. sl st in sl st. Repeat from * 5 times. Finish off; weave in ends.

57 CARCENET
See page 30 in the showcase

This simple and icy design takes its name from a cold gorge wind that blows in the Pyrenees.

Finished diameter: 60mm (2⅜in)
Thread required: 5.5m (6yd)

Foundation ring: ch 6; join with sl st in first ch.
Rnd 1: ch 1 (counts as first dc). 11 dc in ring; join with sl st in initial ch 1.
Rnd 2: ch 3 (counts as first tr). tr in 1 dc. *ch 3. tr in 2 dc. Repeat from * 4 times. ch 3. Join with sl st in 3rd ch of initial ch 3.
Rnd 3: ch 1 (counts as dc). *ch 2. dc in tr. [htr, tr] in next ch 3 space. ch 8, and sl st in top of last tr made to form loop. htr in same ch 3 space.** dc in 1 tr. Repeat from * 4 times, and from * to ** once more. Join with sl st in initial ch 1.
Rnd 4: sl st in next ch 2 space, and ch 1 (counts as dc). *ch 2. Skip dc and htr; and sl st in next tr (at the base of the next loop). [4 dc, ch 2, 4 dc] in ch 8 loop. sl st in the next sl st (at the end of the loop). ch 2.** dc in next ch 2 space. Repeat from * 4 times, and from * to ** once more. Join with sl st in initial ch 1. Finish off; weave in ends.

58 AVALANCHE
See page 30 in the showcase

This hexagonal crystal could pile up with others on a hillside, and then come sliding down in an avalanche of white powder.

Finished diameter: 60mm (2⅜in)
Thread required: 7.3m (8yd)

Foundation ring: ch 6; join with sl st in first ch.
Rnd 1: ch 1 (counts as dc). 11 dc in ring; join with sl st in initial ch 1.
Rnd 2: ch 1 (counts as dc). *ch 3. dc in next dc. Repeat from * 10 times. ch 3. Join with sl st in initial ch 1.
Rnd 3: sl st in next ch 3 space. ch 1 (counts as dc), and dc in same ch 3 space. 2 dc in each of the 11 remaining ch 3 spaces. Join with sl st in initial ch 1.
Rnd 4: ch 1 (counts as dc). *ch 3. dc in next dc. Repeat from * 22 times. ch 3. Join with sl st in initial ch 1.
Rnd 5: sl st in next ch 3 space, and ch 1 (counts as dc). dc in same space. 2 dc in each of the next 3 ch 3 spaces. *ch 4. 2 dc in each of the next 4 ch 3 spaces. Repeat from * 4 times. ch 4. Join with sl st in initial ch 1.
Rnd 6: ch 3 (counts as tr). tr in 1 dc. *ch 1. Skip 1 dc, and dc in 2 dc. ch 1. Skip 1 dc, and tr in 2 dc. [dc, ch 2, dc] in ch 4 point.** tr in next 2 dc. Repeat from * 4 times, and from * to ** once more. Join with sl st in 3rd ch of initial ch 3. Finish off; weave in ends.

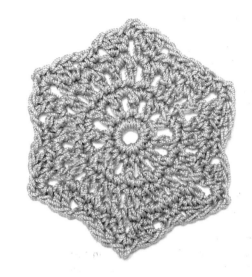

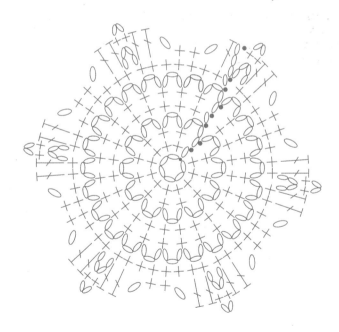

59 NORTHERN NANNY
See page 31 in the showcase

This pattern gets its colorful name from a cold hail and wind storm in northern England.

Finished diameter: 79mm (3⅛in)
Thread required: 7.3m (8yd)

Foundation ring: ch 6; join with sl st in first ch.
Rnd 1: ch 1 (counts as dc). 11 dc in ring; join with sl st in initial ch 1.
Rnd 2: ch 1 (counts as dc). *ch 4. dc in next dc. Repeat from * 10 times. ch 4. Join with sl st in initial ch 1.
Rnd 3: sl st in next ch 4 loop. ch 1 (counts as dc). 1 dc in same loop. *ch 1. 2 dc in next ch 4 loop. Repeat from * 10 times. ch 1. Join with sl st in initial ch 1.
Rnd 4: ch 1 (counts as dc). dc in dc. *dc in ch 1 space. dc in 1 dc. ch 3. dc in next dc. dc in ch 1 space. ** dc in 2 dc. Repeat from * 4 times, and from * to ** once more. Join with sl st in initial ch 1.
Rnd 5: ch 1 (counts as dc). *ch 3. dc in next dc. ch 2. 2 dc in next ch 3 point. ch 6, and sl st in 6th ch from hook to form loop. ch 10, and sl st in 10th ch from hook. ch 6, and sl st in 6th ch from hook. 2 dc in same ch 3 point as last dc. ch 2.** Skip 2 dc, and dc in 1 dc. Repeat from * 4 times, and from * to ** once more. Join with sl st in initial ch 1. Finish off; weave in ends.

60 MISTRAL
See page 32 in the showcase

This light, star-shaped flake might have been whipped up by the Mistral, a cold, dry wind in France, which is particularly violent in the winter.

Finished diameter: 67mm (2⅝in)
Thread required: 4.6m (5yd)

Foundation ring: ch 6; join with sl st in first ch.
Rnd 1: ch 1 (counts as first dc). 11 dc in ring; join with sl st in initial ch 1.
Rnd 2: ch 1 (counts as dc). dc in 1 dc. *ch 5. dc in 2 dc. Repeat from * 4 times. ch 5. Join with sl st in initial ch 1.
Rnd 3: ch 1 (counts as dc). *ch 4, and sl st in 4th ch from hook to form picot. dc in next dc. ch 4. dtr in top of ch 5 point. [ch 6, and sl st in 6th ch from hook] 3 times. sl st in top of last dtr made. ch 4.** dc in next dc. Repeat from * 4 times, and from * to ** once more. Join with sl st in initial ch 1. Finish off; weave in ends.

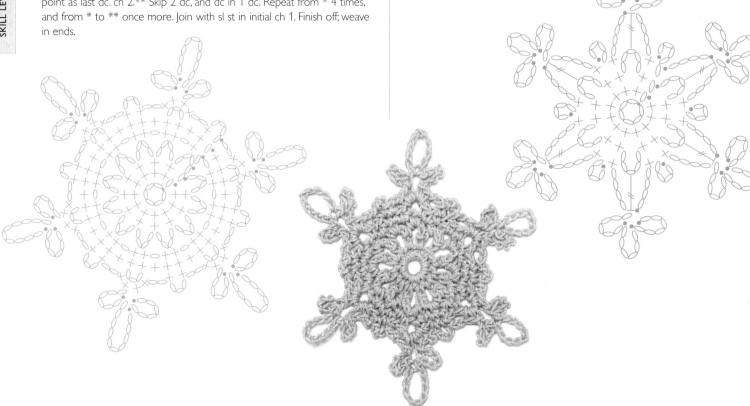

61 CIRQUE GLACIER
See page 33 in the showcase

This curvy flake would be at home resting on a cirque glacier, a small glacier in a mountain hollow.

Finished diameter: 70mm (2¾in)
Thread required: 7.3m (8yd)

Foundation ring: ch 6; join with sl st in first ch.
Rnd 1: ch 1 (counts as first dc). 11 dc in ring; join with sl st in initial ch 1.
Rnd 2: ch 1 (counts as first dc). *[dc, ch 6, dc] in 1 dc.** dc in 1 dc. Repeat from * 4 times, and from * to ** once more. Join with sl st in initial ch 1.
Rnd 3: ch 1 (counts as dc). *[4 dc, ch 2, 4 dc] in next ch 6 loop.** Skip 1 dc (at the bottom of the loop). dc in 1 dc (halfway between loops). Repeat from *4 times, and from * to ** once more. Join with sl st in initial ch 1.
Rnd 4: ch 1 (counts as dc). *ch 5. [tr, ch 2, tr] in next ch 2 point. ch 5.** Skip 4 dc, and dc in 1 dc. Repeat from * 4 times, and from * to ** once more. Join with sl st in initial ch 1.
Rnd 5: sl st in ch 5 space. ch 1 (counts as dc). 3 dc in same ch 5 space. *dc in tr. dc in ch 2 point. ch 4, and sl st in 4th ch from hook to form picot. dc in same ch 2 point. dc in tr.** 4 dc in each of the next 2 ch 5 spaces. Repeat from * 4 times, and from * to ** once more. 4 dc in next ch 5 space. Join with sl st in initial ch 1. Finish off; weave in ends.

62 WINTER SOLSTICE
See page 33 in the showcase

This fragile-looking star could have drifted to earth on the winter solstice, the shortest day of the year.

Finished diameter: 76mm (3in)
Thread required: 5.5m (6yd)

Foundation ring: ch 6; join with sl st in first ch.
Rnd 1: ch 1 (counts as dc). 11 dc in ring; join with sl st in initial ch 1.
Rnd 2: ch 1 (counts as dc). *[tr; ch 3, tr] in next dc.** dc in 1 dc. Repeat from * 4 times, and from * to ** once more. Join with sl st in initial ch 1.
Rnd 3: ch 1 (counts as dc). ch 4, and sl st in 4th ch from hook to form picot. dc in same stitch as initial sl st (the stitch that joined Rnd 2). *2 dc in next ch 3 point. ch 9, and sl st in 6th ch from hook. ch 8, and sl st in 8th ch from hook. ch 6, and sl st in 6th ch from hook. sl st in 3rd ch of ch 9. ch 2. 2 dc in same ch 3 point as last dc.** Skip tr, and dc in next dc. ch 4, and sl st in 4th ch from hook. dc in same dc as last dc. Repeat from * 4 times, and from * to ** once more. Join with sl st in initial ch 1. Finish off; weave in ends.

63 SUESTADA
See page 33 in the showcase

A Suestada is a strong, winter windstorm on the east coast of South America.

Finished diameter: 83mm (3¼in)
Thread required: 7.3m (8yd)

Foundation ring: ch 6; join with sl st in first ch.
Rnd 1: ch 1 (counts as dc). 11 dc in ring; join with sl st in initial ch 1.
Rnd 2: ch 1 (counts as dc). *ch 6. skip 1 dc, and dc in 1 dc. Repeat from * 4 times. ch 6. Join with sl st in initial ch 1.
Rnd 3: ch 1 (counts as dc). *[2 dc, tr; ch 1, tr; 2 dc] in next ch 6 space.** dc in next dc. Repeat from * 4 times, and from * to ** once more. Join with sl st in initial ch 1.
Rnd 4: sl st in 2 dc. ch 1 (counts as dc). *dc in tr. [dc, ch 2, dc] in ch 1 point. dc in tr; dc in 1 dc. ch 3.** Skip 3 dc, and dc in 1 dc. Repeat from * 4 times, and from * to ** once more. Join with sl st in initial ch 1.
Rnd 5: ch 1 (counts as dc). dc in 2 dc. *dc in ch 2 point. ch 6, and sl st in 6th ch from hook to form loop. ch 10, and sl st in 10th ch from hook. ch 6, and sl st in 6th ch from hook. dc in same ch 2 point as last dc. dc in 3 dc. dc in ch 3 space.** dc in 3 dc. Repeat from * 4 times, and from * to ** once more. Join with sl st in initial ch 1. Finish off; weave in ends.

64 ELVEGUST
See page 32 in the showcase

The namesake of this regal design is a cold and squally wind in the fjords of Norway.

Finished diameter: 79mm (3⅛in)
Thread required: 8.2m (9yd)

Foundation ring: ch 6; join with sl st in first ch.
Rnd 1: ch 1 (counts as first dc). 11 dc in ring; join with sl st in initial ch 1.
Rnd 2: ch 1 (counts as dc). dc in 1 dc. *ch 3. dc in 2 dc. Repeat from * 4 times. ch 3. Join with sl st in initial ch 1.
Rnd 3: sl st in dc, and in ch 3 space. ch 1 (counts as dc). *ch 5. dc in next ch 3 point. Repeat from * 4 times. ch 5. Join with sl st in initial ch 1.
Rnd 4: sl st in ch 5 space. ch 1 (counts as dc). 5 dc in same ch 5 space. *ch 3. 6 dc in next ch 5 space. Repeat from * 4 times. ch 3. Join with sl st in initial ch 1.
Rnd 5: sl st in 1 dc. ch 1 (counts as dc). dc in 3 dc. *ch 1. Skip 1 dc. [2 tr, ch 3, 2 tr] in ch 3 point. ch 1.** Skip 1 dc, and dc in 4 dc. Repeat from * 4 times, and from * to ** once more. Join with sl st in initial ch 1.
Rnd 6: sl st in 3 dc, and in ch 1 space. ch 1 (counts as dc). *dc in 2 tr. 2 dc in ch 3 point. ch 6, and sl st in 6th ch from hook to form loop. 2 dc in same ch 3 point. dc in 2 tr, and in ch 1 space. ch 3.** Skip 4 dc, and dc in next ch 1 space. Repeat from * 4 times, and from * to ** once more. Join with sl st in initial ch 1. Finish off; weave in ends.

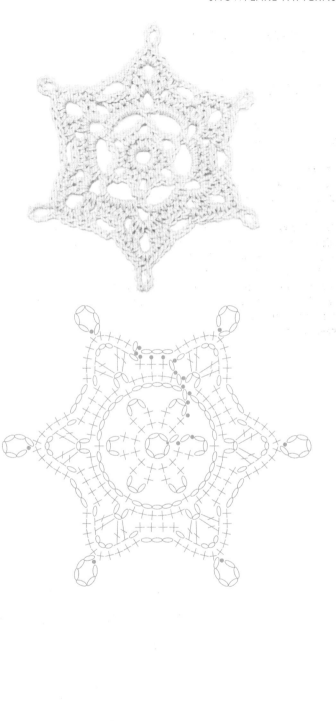

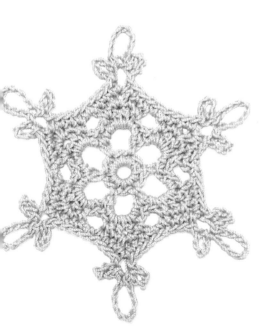

SKILL LEVEL INTERMEDIATE

65 SEA ICE I
See page 32 in the showcase

This tiny flake and its heavier companion might be found resting on an area of sea ice.

Finished diameter: 57mm (2¼in)
Thread required: 4.6m (5yd)

Foundation ring: ch 6; join with sl st in first ch.
Rnd 1: ch 3 (counts as first tr). 11 tr in ring; join with sl st in 3rd ch of initial ch 3.
Rnd 2: ch 1 (counts as dc). *[tr, ch 2, tr] in 1 tr.** dc in 1 tr. Repeat from * 4 times, and from * to ** once more. Join with sl st in initial ch 1.
Rnd 3: sl st in tr, and in ch 2 space. ch 1 (counts as dc). Make loop cluster: {ch 6, and sl st in 6th ch from hook for picot. ch 8, and sl st in 8th ch from hook. ch 6, and sl st in 6th ch from hook. *Loop cluster complete.*} sl st in ch 1 (which counted as the first dc). dc in same ch 2 space. *ch 4; dc in next ch 2 space. Repeat between {} to make loop cluster. sl st in top of last dc made. dc in same ch 2 space as last dc. Repeat from * 4 times. ch 4; join with sl st in initial ch 1. Finish off; weave in ends.

66 SEA ICE II
See page 33 in the showcase

This pattern adds a round of double crochets to the outer edge of Sea Ice I, transforming the fine, lacy flake into a more substantial hexagonal crystal.

Finished diameter: 57mm (2¼in)
Thread required: 6.4m (7yd)

Foundation ring: ch 6; join with sl st in first ch.
Rnd 1: ch 3 (counts as first tr). 11 tr in ring; join with sl st in 3rd ch of initial ch 3.
Rnd 2: ch 1 (counts as dc). *[tr, ch 2, tr] in 1 tr.** dc in 1 tr. Repeat from * 4 times, and from * to ** once more. Join with sl st in initial ch 1.
Rnd 3: sl st in tr, and in ch 2 space. ch 1 (counts as dc). Make loop cluster: {ch 6, and sl st in 6th ch from hook for picot. ch 8, and sl st in 8th ch from hook. ch 6, and sl st in 6th ch from hook. *Loop cluster complete.*} sl st in ch 1 (which counted as the first dc). dc in same ch 2 space. *ch 4, dc in next ch 2 space. Repeat between {} to make loop cluster. sl st in top of last dc made. dc in same ch 2 space as last dc. Repeat from * 4 times. ch 4. Join with sl st in initial ch 1. Finish off; weave in ends.
Rnd 4: sl st in first 2 ch of ch 6 loop. sl st in loop, and ch 1 (counts as dc). 2 dc in same loop. *[2 dc, ch 2, 2 dc] in next ch 8 loop. 3 dc in next ch 6 loop.** Moving to the next cluster of loops, 3 dc in first ch 6 loop. Repeat from * 4 times, and from * to ** once more. Join with sl st in initial ch 1. Finish off; weave in ends.

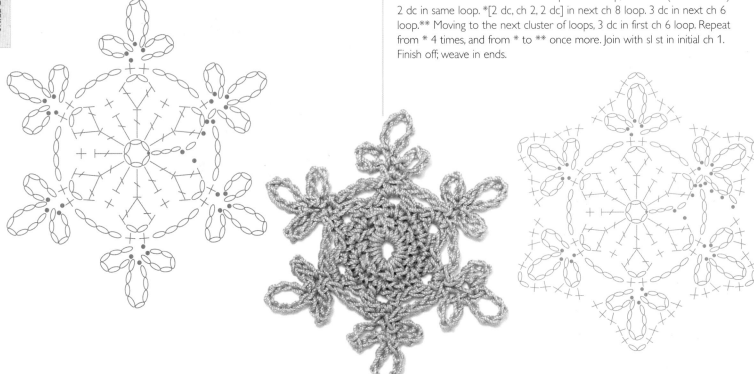

67 N'ADCHI
See page 32 in the showcase

This exquisite flake is named after a northeasterly wind that occurs in the winter on the Iranian coast of the Persian Gulf.

Finished diameter: 86mm (3⅜in)
Thread required: 11m (12yd)

Foundation ring: ch 6; join with sl st in first ch.
Rnd 1: ch 1 (counts as first dc). 11 dc in ring; join with sl st in initial ch 1.
Rnd 2: ch 1 (counts as dc). dc in 1 dc. *ch 5. dc in 2 dc. Repeat from * 4 times. ch 5. Join with sl st in initial ch 1.
Rnd 3: sl st in 1 dc, and in ch 5 point. ch 1 (counts as dc). 2 dc in same point. ch 3, and 3 dc in same ch 5 point. *ch 1. [3 dc, ch 3, 3 dc] in next ch 5 point. Repeat from * 4 times. ch 1. Join with sl st in initial ch 1.
Rnd 4: sl st in 2 dc, and in ch 3 point. ch 1 (counts as dc). dc in same ch 3 point, ch 2, and 2 dc in same point. *ch 2. tr in next ch 1 space (halfway between points). ch 2.** [2 dc, ch 2, 2 dc] in next ch 3 point. Repeat from * 4 times, and from * to ** once more. Join with sl st in initial ch 1.
Rnd 5: sl st in 1 dc, and ch 3 (counts as tr). *[tr, ch 2, tr] in ch 2 point. tr in 1 dc. Skip 1 dc. 2 tr in each of the next 2 ch 2 spaces.** Skip 1 dc, and tr in 1 dc. Repeat from * 4 times, and from * to ** once more. Join with sl st in 3rd ch of initial ch 3.
Rnd 6: ch 1 (counts as dc). *ch 2. dc in next tr. ch 2. [dc, ch 8, dc] in ch 2 point. [ch 2, dc] in each of the next 2 tr. ch 5, and sl st in 4th ch from hook to form picot. ch 1.** Skip 4 tr, and dc in 1 tr. Repeat from * 4 times, and from * to ** once more. Join with sl st in initial ch 1. Finish off; weave in ends.

SKILL LEVEL INTERMEDIATE

68 CANDLE ICE
See page 32 in the showcase

This little snowflake might come to rest on a pile of candle ice – lake or sea ice that has disintegrated into a pile of candle-shaped cylinders.

Finished diameter: 60mm (2⅜in)
Thread required: 5.5m (6yd)

Foundation ring: ch 6; join with sl st in first ch.
Rnd 1: ch 3 (counts as tr). 11 tr in ring; join with sl st in 3rd ch of initial ch 3.
Rnd 2: ch 1 (counts as dc). dc in 1 tr. *ch 4. dc in 2 tr. Repeat from * 4 times. ch 4. Join with sl st in initial ch 1.
Rnd 3: ch 1 (counts as dc). dc in dc. *[2 dc, ch 3, 2 dc] in ch 4 space.** dc in 2 dc. Repeat from * 4 times, and from * to ** once more. Join with sl st in initial ch 1.
Rnd 4: ch 1 (counts as dc). dc in 1 dc. *ch 4. Skip 2 dc, and tr in next ch 3 point. ch 4.** Skip 2 dc, and dc in 2 dc. Repeat from * 4 times, and from * to ** once more. Join with sl st in initial ch 1.
Rnd 5: sl st in dc, and in next ch 4 space. ch 1 (counts as dc). 3 dc in same ch 4 space. *[dc, ch 4, dc] in tr.** 4 dc in each of the next 2 ch 4 spaces. Repeat from * 4 times, and from * to ** once more. 4 dc in ch 4 space. Join with sl st in initial ch 1. Finish off; weave in ends.

69 PLANE DENDRITE
See page 33 in the showcase

Dendrite means 'treelike', and plane dendrites are snowflakes like this one, with intricate, branching arms.

Finished diameter: 73mm (2⅞in)
Thread required: 5.5m (6yd)

Foundation ring: ch 6; join with sl st in first ch.
Rnd 1: ch 1 (counts as first dc). 11 dc in ring; join with sl st in initial ch 1.
Rnd 2: ch 1 (counts as dc). dc in 1 dc. *ch 3. dc in 2 dc. Repeat from * 4 times. ch 3. Join with sl st in initial ch 1.
Rnd 3: ch 1 (counts as dc). dc in dc. *dc in ch 3 point. ch 7, and sl st in 6th ch from hook to form picot. ch 6, and sl st in 5th ch from hook. ch 5, and sl st in 4th ch from hook. [ch 4, and sl st in 4th ch from hook] twice. sl st in 1st ch of last ch 5. ch 5, and sl st in 5th ch from hook. sl st in 1st ch of last ch 6. ch 6, and sl st in 6th ch from hook. sl st in 1st ch of last ch 7. dc in same ch 3 point as last dc.** dc in 2 dc. Repeat from * 4 times, and from * to ** once more. Join with sl st in initial ch 1. Finish off; weave in ends.

70 WHITEOUT
See page 34 in the showcase

Lifted by a high wind, crystals like this one can obscure visibility with a curtain of snow.

Finished diameter: 89mm (3½in)
Thread required: 11m (12yd)

Foundation ring: ch 6; join with sl st in first ch.
Rnd 1: ch 3 (counts as tr). 11 tr in ring; join with sl st in 3rd ch of initial ch 3.
Rnd 2: ch 1 (counts as dc). dc in 1 tr. *ch 4. dc in 2 tr. Repeat from * 4 times. ch 4. Join with sl st in initial ch 1.
Rnd 3: sl st in dc, and in ch 4 space. ch 1 (counts as dc). 2 dc in same ch 4 space. ch 2, and 3 dc in same ch 4 space. *ch 1. [3 dc, ch 2, 3dc] in the next ch 4 space. Repeat from * 4 times. ch 1. Join with sl st in initial ch 1.
Rnd 4: sl st in 2 dc, and in ch 2 point. ch 1 (counts as dc). *ch 4. tr in next ch 1 space (halfway between points). ch 4.** dc in next ch 2 point. Repeat from * 4 times, and from * to ** once more. Join with sl st in initial ch 1.
Rnd 5: sl st in ch 4 space. ch 3 (counts as tr). 3 tr in same space. *tr in tr. 4 tr in next ch 4 space.** [tr, ch 2, tr] in dc. 4 tr in next ch 4 space. Repeat from * 4 times, and from * to ** once more. [tr, ch 2, tr] in sl st (the stitch that joined Rnd 4). Join with sl st in 3rd ch of initial ch 3.
Rnd 6: ch 1 (counts as dc). dc in 3 tr. *ch 4, and sl st in 4th ch from hook to form picot. Skip 1 tr, and dc in 4 tr. [dc, ch 4, dc, ch 8, dc, ch 4, dc] in ch 2 point.** Skip 1 tr, and dc in 4 tr. Repeat from * 4 times, and from * to ** once more. Join with sl st in initial ch 1. Finish off; weave in ends.

SKILL LEVEL INTERMEDIATE

71 TUNDRA
See page 35 in the showcase

This frozen star would be well-suited to the tundra, an area near the poles (or high in the mountains) where no trees grow – only moss, lichen and small plants.

Finished diameter: 73mm (2⅞in)
Thread required: 6.4m (7yd)

Foundation ring: ch 6; join with sl st in first ch.
Rnd 1: ch 3 (counts as tr). 1 tr in ring. *ch 2. 2 tr in ring. Repeat from * 4 times. ch 2. Join with sl st in 3rd ch of initial ch 3.
Rnd 2: ch 1 (counts as dc). dc in tr. *[dc, ch 4, dc] in ch 2 space.** dc in 2 tr. Repeat from * 4 times, and from * to ** once more. Join with sl st in initial ch 1.
Rnd 3: sl st in 2 dc, and in ch 4 point. ch 1 (counts as dc). 2 dc in same ch 4 point. ch 2. 3 dc in same point. *ch 3. [3 dc, ch 2, 3 dc] in next ch 4 point. Repeat from * 4 times. ch 3. Join with sl st in initial ch 1.
Rnd 4: ch 1 (counts as dc). dc in 2 dc. *dc in ch 2 point. ch 5, and sl st in 4th ch from hook to form picot. [ch 4, and sl st in 4th ch from hook] 2 times. sl st in 1st ch of ch 5. dc in same ch 2 point as last dc. dc in 3 dc. 1 dc in ch 3 space. ch 3 and join in 3rd ch from hook to form picot. dc in same ch 3 space as last dc.** dc in 3 dc. Repeat from * 4 times, and from * to ** once more. Join with sl st in initial ch 1. Finish off; weave in ends.

72 CIERZO
See page 34 in the showcase

'Cierzo' is a Spanish term for the Mistral, a cold, dry wind that blows in France and parts of Spain.

Finished diameter: 70mm (2¾in)
Thread required: 7.3m (8yd)

Foundation ring: ch 6; join with sl st in first ch.
Rnd 1: ch 1 (counts as first dc). 11 dc in ring; join with sl st in initial ch 1.
Rnd 2: ch 1 (counts as dc). dc in 1 dc. *ch 3. dc in 2 dc. Repeat from * 4 times. ch 3. Join with sl st in initial ch 1.
Rnd 3: sl st in dc, and in ch 3 point. ch 3 (counts as tr). tr in same ch 3 point. ch 3; 2 tr in same ch 3 point. [2 tr, ch 3, 2 tr] in each of the 5 remaining ch 3 points. Join with sl st in 3rd ch of initial ch 3.
Rnd 4: ch 1 (counts as dc). dc in tr. *[htr, tr, ch 5, tr, htr] in ch 3 point.** dc in 4 tr. Repeat from * 4 times, and from * to ** once more. dc in 2 tr. Join with sl st in initial ch 1.
Rnd 5: sl st in dc. ch 1 (counts as dc). *dc in htr, and in tr. [3 dc, ch 4, 3 dc] in ch 5 point. dc in tr, in htr, and in 1 dc. ch 4, and sl st in 4th ch from hook to form picot.** Skip 2 dc, and dc in 1 dc. Repeat from * 4 times, and from * to ** once more. Join with sl st in initial ch 1. Finish off; weave in ends.

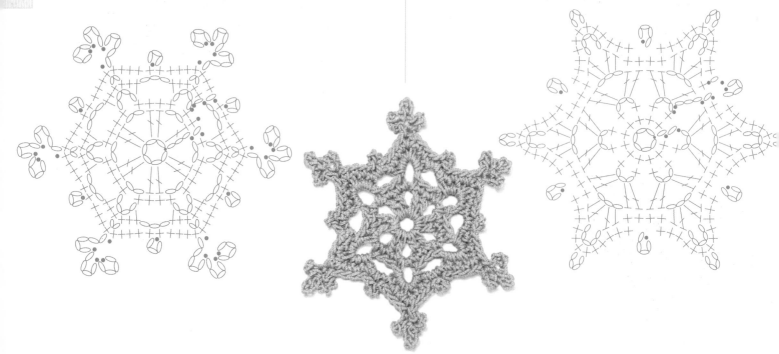

73 SANSAR
See page 35 in the showcase

This snowflake's title comes from a cold, northwest wind in Iran, whose memorable name means 'icy wind of death'.

Finished diameter: 89mm (3½in)
Thread required: 8.2m (9yd)

Foundation ring: ch 6; join with sl st in first ch.
Rnd 1: ch 1 (counts as first dc). 11 dc in ring; join with sl st in initial ch 1.
Rnd 2: ch 1 (counts as dc). dc in 1 dc. *ch 5. dc in 2 dc. Repeat from * 4 times. ch 5. Join with sl st in initial ch 1.
Rnd 3: sl st in 1 dc, and in ch 5 point. ch 1 (counts as dc). 2 dc in same point. ch 3, and 3 dc in same ch 5 point. *ch 1. [3 dc, ch 3, 3 dc] in next ch 5 point. Repeat from * 4 times. ch 1. Join with sl st in initial ch 1.
Rnd 4: sl st in 2 dc, and in ch 3 point. ch 3 (counts as tr). *ch 5. tr in next ch 1 space (halfway between points). ch 5.** tr in next ch 3 point. Repeat from * 4 times, and from * to ** once more. Join with sl st in 3rd ch of initial ch 3.
Rnd 5: ch 1 (counts as dc). Make loop cluster: {ch 7, and sl st in 6th ch from hook. ch 8, and sl st in 8th ch from hook. ch 6, and sl st in 6th ch from hook. sl st in 1st ch of ch 7. *Loop cluster complete.*} dc in same stitch as initial sl st (the stitch that joined Rnd 4). *ch 2. dc in ch 5 space. ch 2. [dc, ch 4, dc] in next tr. ch 2. dc in next ch 5 space. ch 2.** dc in next tr. Repeat between {} to make loop cluster. dc in same tr as last dc. Repeat from * 4 times, and from * to ** once more. Join with sl st in initial ch 1. Finish off; weave in ends.

74 BLIZZARD
See page 34 in the showcase

This fanciful snowflake might land on your windowsill, during a midwinter blizzard.

Finished diameter: 70mm (2¾in)
Thread required: 8.2m (9yd)

Foundation ring: ch 6; join with sl st in first ch.
Rnd 1: ch 1 (counts as first dc). 11 dc in ring; join with sl st in initial ch 1.
Rnd 2: *ch 5. dtr in 1 dc. ch 5.** sl st in next dc. Repeat from * 4 times, and from * to ** once more. Join with sl st in sl st.
Rnd 3: sl st in ch 5 space. ch 1 (counts as dc). 3 dc in same ch 5 space. *ch 2. Skip dtr. 4 dc in each of the next 2 ch 5 spaces. Repeat from * 4 times. ch 2. 4 dc in next ch 5 space. Join with sl st in initial ch 1.
Rnd 4: sl st in 3 dc, and in ch 2 point. ch 1 (counts as dc). ch 8. dc in same ch 2 point. *ch 7. [dc, ch 8, dc] in next ch 2 point. Repeat from * 4 times. ch 7. Join with sl st in initial ch 1.
Rnd 5: sl st in next ch 8 loop. ch 1 (counts as dc). 3 dc in same ch 8 loop. ch 2, and 4 dc in same loop. *[dc, htr, tr] in next ch 7 space. ch 4, and sl st in 4th ch from hook to form picot. [tr, htr, dc] in same ch 7 space.** [4 dc, ch 2, 4 dc] in next ch 8 loop. Repeat from * 4 times, and from * to ** once more. Join with sl st in initial ch 1. Finish off; weave in ends.

75 BOULBIE
See page 35 in the showcase

Beautiful in its simplicity, this large flake is named after a violent winter wind in the Ariège valley in France.

Finished diameter: 83mm (3¼in)
Thread required: 8.2m (9yd)

Foundation ring: ch 6; join with sl st in first ch.
Rnd 1: ch 1 (counts as first dc). 11 dc in ring; join with sl st in initial ch 1.
Rnd 2: ch 3 (counts as tr). tr in same stitch as last sl st (the stitch that joined Rnd 1). 2 tr in each of the 11 dc. Join with sl st in 3rd ch of initial ch 3.
Rnd 3: ch 1 (counts as dc). *ch 4. Skip 1 tr, and dc in 1 tr. Repeat from * 10 times. ch 4. Join with sl st in initial ch 1.
Rnd 4: sl st in ch 4 space. ch 1 (counts as dc). 3 dc in same ch 4 space. *ch 2. 4 dc in each of the next 2 ch 4 spaces. Repeat from * 4 times. ch 2. 4 dc in next ch 4 space. Join with sl st in initial ch 1.
Rnd 5: sl st in 1 dc. ch 1 (counts as dc). dc in 2 dc. *In the chain 2 point, work the following sequence: [tr, dtr; ch 10, and sl st in 10th ch from hook to form loop; dtr, tr]. dc in 3 dc. ch 1.** Skip 2 dc, and dc in 3 dc. Repeat from * 4 times, and from * to ** once more. Join with sl st in initial ch 1. Finish off; weave in ends.

76 POLARIS
See page 34 in the showcase

On a winter evening, this large, branching snowflake might catch a glimmer of light from Polaris, the north pole star.

Finished diameter: 105mm (4⅛in)
Thread required: 11m (12yd)

Foundation ring: ch 6; join with sl st in first ch.
Rnd 1: ch 1 (counts as first dc). 11 dc in ring; join with sl st in initial ch 1.
Rnd 2: ch 1 (counts as dc). dc in 1 dc. *ch 3. dc in 2 dc. Repeat from * 4 times. ch 3. Join with sl st in initial ch 1.
Rnd 3: sl st in dc, and in ch 3 point. ch 3 (counts as tr). tr in same ch 3 point. ch 3; 2 tr in same ch 3 point. [2 tr, ch 3, 2 tr] in each of the 5 remaining ch 3 points. Join with sl st in 3rd ch of initial ch 3.
Rnd 4: ch 3 (counts as tr). tr in tr. *[2 tr, ch 4, 2 tr] in ch 3 point.** tr in 4 tr. Repeat from * 4 times, and from * to ** once more. tr in 2 tr. Join with sl st in 3rd ch of initial ch 3.
Rnd 5: ch 1 (counts as dc). dc in 1 tr. *ch 4, and sl st in 4th ch from hook to form picot. dc in 2 tr. 2 dc in ch 4 point. ch 8, and sl st in 7th ch from hook. ch 6, and sl st in 5th ch from hook. ch 7, and sl st in 7th ch from hook. ch 5, and sl st in 5th ch from hook. sl st in 1st ch of last ch 6. ch 7, and sl st in 7th ch from hook. sl st in 1st ch of last ch 8. 2 dc in same ch 4 point as last dc. dc in 2 tr. ch 4, and sl st in 4th ch from hook.** dc in 4 tr. Repeat from * 4 times, and from * to ** once more. dc in 2 tr. Join with sl st in initial ch 1. Finish off; weave in ends.

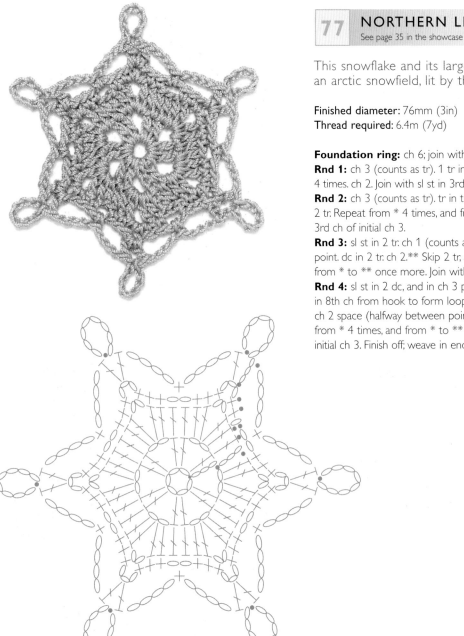

77 NORTHERN LIGHTS I
See page 35 in the showcase

This snowflake and its larger cousin would be at home in an arctic snowfield, lit by the shimmering Northern Lights.

Finished diameter: 76mm (3in)
Thread required: 6.4m (7yd)

Foundation ring: ch 6; join with sl st in first ch.
Rnd 1: ch 3 (counts as tr). 1 tr in ring. *ch 2. 2 tr in ring. Repeat from * 4 times. ch 2. Join with sl st in 3rd ch of initial ch 3.
Rnd 2: ch 3 (counts as tr). tr in tr. *[2 tr, ch 2, 2 tr] in ch 2 space.** tr in 2 tr. Repeat from * 4 times, and from * to ** once more. Join with sl st in 3rd ch of initial ch 3.
Rnd 3: sl st in 2 tr. ch 1 (counts as dc). dc in next tr. *[dc, ch 3, dc] in ch 2 point. dc in 2 tr. ch 2.** Skip 2 tr, and dc in 2 tr. Repeat from * 4 times, and from * to ** once more. Join with sl st in initial ch 1.
Rnd 4: sl st in 2 dc, and in ch 3 point. ch 3 (counts as tr). *ch 8, and sl st in 8th ch from hook to form loop. tr in same ch 3 point. ch 4. dc in next ch 2 space (halfway between points). ch 4.** tr in next ch 3 point. Repeat from * 4 times, and from * to ** once more. Join with sl st in 3rd ch of initial ch 3. Finish off; weave in ends.

78 NORTHERN LIGHTS II

See page 35 in the showcase

The Northern Lights snowflakes are more complex than the other sequenced snowflakes in this collection, but the principle is the same – added ornamentation around the edges produces a very different appearance, and the fine and simple Northern Lights I becomes the ornate Northern Lights II.

Finished diameter: 89mm (3½in)
Thread required: 11.9m (13yd)

Foundation ring: ch 6; join with sl st in first ch.
Rnd 1: ch 3 (counts as tr). 1 tr in ring. *ch 2. 2 tr in ring. Repeat from * 4 times. ch 2. Join with sl st in 3rd ch of initial ch 3.
Rnd 2: ch 3 (counts as tr). tr in tr. *[2 tr, ch 2, 2 tr] in ch 2 space.** tr in 2 tr. Repeat from * 4 times, and from * to ** once more. Join with sl st in 3rd ch of initial ch 3.
Rnd 3: sl st in 2 tr. ch 1 (counts as dc). dc in next tr. *[dc, ch 3, dc] in ch 2 point. dc in 2 tr. ch 2.** Skip 2 tr, and dc in 2 tr. Repeat from * 4 times, and from * to ** once more. Join with sl st in initial ch 1.
Rnd 4: sl st in 2 dc, and in ch 3 point. ch 3 (counts as tr). *ch 8, and sl st in 8th ch from hook to form loop. tr in same ch 3 point as last tr. ch 4. dc in next ch 2 space (halfway between points). ch 4.** tr in next ch 3 point. Repeat from * 4 times, and from * to ** once more. Join with sl st in 3rd ch of initial ch 3.
Rnd 5: ch 1 (counts as dc). *7 dc in ch 8 loop. dc in tr. ch 4. tr in next dc (halfway between points). ch 4.** dc in next tr. Repeat from * 4 times, and from * to ** once more. Join with sl st in initial ch 1.
Rnd 6: sl st in 1 dc. ch 1 (counts as dc). dc in 2 dc. *[dc, ch 3, dc] in next dc (at the top of the loop). dc in 3 dc. Skip 1 dc. 4 dc in each of the next 2 ch 4 spaces.** Skip 1 dc, and dc in 3 dc. Repeat from * 4 times, and from * to ** once more. Join with sl st in initial ch 1. Finish off; weave in ends.

79 GUXEN
See page 37 in the showcase

This lovely flake might be carried by the Guxen, a cold wind that blows in the Swiss Alps.

Finished diameter: 70mm (2¾in)
Thread required: 7.3m (8yd)

Foundation ring: ch 6; join with sl st in first ch.
Rnd 1: ch 1 (counts as first dc). 11 dc in ring; join with sl st in initial ch 1.
Rnd 2: ch 3 (counts as tr). tr in 1 dc. *ch 5. tr in 2 dc. Repeat from * 4 times. ch 5. Join with sl st in 3rd ch of initial ch 3.
Rnd 3: ch 1 (counts as dc). *ch 2. dc in tr. [dc, htr, tr, ch 4, tr, htr, dc] in ch 5 space.** dc in 1 tr. Repeat from * 4 times, and from * to ** once more. Join with sl st in initial ch 1.
Rnd 4: sl st in ch 2 point. ch 1 (counts as dc). *ch 4. [dc, ch 1, 2 tr, ch 1, dc] in next ch 4 point (at top of next petal). ch 4.** dc in next ch 2 point (halfway between petals). Repeat from * 4 times, and from * to ** once more. Join with sl st in initial ch 1.
Rnd 5: ch 1 (counts as dc). *ch 4. dc in next dc. dc in ch 1 space, and in tr. ch 1. dc in tr, in ch 1 space, and in dc. ch 4.** dc in next dc (halfway between petals). Repeat from * 4 times, and from * to ** once more. Join with sl st in initial ch 1. Finish off; weave in ends.

80 SEA SMOKE
See page 36 in the showcase

This diaphanous design takes its name from a term for the fog formed when very cold air passes over warmer water.

Finished diameter: 86mm (3⅜in)
Thread required: 7.3m (8yd)

Foundation ring: ch 6; join with sl st in first ch.
Rnd 1: ch 3 (counts as tr). *ch 2. dtr in ring. ch 2.** tr in ring. Repeat from * 4 times, and from * to ** once more. Join with sl st in 3rd ch of initial ch 3.
Rnd 2: ch 1 (counts as dc). *ch 2. [dc, ch 2, dc] in next dtr. ch 2.** dc in next tr. Repeat from * 4 times, and from * to ** once more. Join with sl st in initial ch 1.
Rnd 3: ch 1 (counts as dc). *ch 4. tr in next ch 2 point. ch 6, and sl st in top of last tr made, to form loop. ch 4.** Skip 1 dc, and dc in next dc (halfway between points). Repeat from * 4 times, and from * to ** once more. Join with sl st in initial ch 1.
Rnd 4: ch 1 (counts as dc). *ch 4. [2 dc, ch 4, dc, ch 6, dc, ch 4, 2 dc] in next ch 6 loop. ch 4.** dc in next dc (halfway between loops). Repeat from * 4 times, and from * to ** once more. Join with sl st in initial ch 1. Finish off; weave in ends.

ICE FEATHERS
See page 36 in the showcase

The feathery edges of this snowflake look like ice feathers, a name given to thick, feathery frost formations.

Finished diameter: 83mm (3¼in)
Thread required: 11.9m (13yd)

Foundation ring: ch 6; join with sl st in first ch.
Rnd 1: ch 5 (counts as dtr). dtr in ring. *ch 2; 2 dtr in ring. Repeat from * 4 times. ch 2; join with sl st in 5th ch of initial ch 5.
Rnd 2: ch 5 (counts as dtr). dtr in dtr. *[2 dtr; ch 2, 2 dtr] in ch 2 space.** dtr in 2 dtr. Repeat from * 4 times, and from * to ** once more. Join with sl st in 5th ch of initial ch 5.
Rnd 3: ch 1 (counts as dc). ch 2. dc in next 3 dtr. *[dc, ch 2, dc] in ch 2 space.** dc in 3 dtr; ch 2; dc in 3 dtr. Repeat from * 4 times, and from * to ** once more. dc in 2 dtr. Join with sl st in initial ch 1.
Rnd 4: sl st in next ch 2 point. ch 1 (counts as dc). ch 6. dc in same ch 2 point to form loop. *ch 6. [dc, ch 10, dc] in next ch 2 point to form loop. ch 6.** [dc, ch 6, dc] in next ch 2 point. Repeat from * 4 times, and from * to ** once more. Join with sl st in initial ch 1.
Rnd 5: sl st in 1 ch of ch 6 loop. sl st in loop; ch 1 (counts as dc). dc in same loop; ch 2; 2 dc in same loop. *4 dc in ch 6 space. [4 dc, ch 2, 4 dc] in ch 10 loop. 4 dc in next ch 6 space.** [2 dc, ch 2, 2 dc] in ch 6 loop. Repeat from * 4 times and from * to ** once more. Join with sl st in initial ch 1. Finish off; weave in ends.

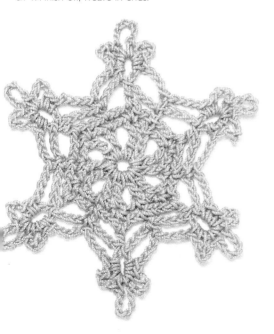

82 CRYSTALLINE FROST
See page 37 in the showcase

This hexagonal design takes its name from a term for frost with a simple crystalline structure.

Finished diameter: 60mm (2⅜in)
Thread required: 8.2m (9yd)

Foundation ring: ch 6; join with sl st in first ch.
Rnd 1: ch 1 (counts as first dc). 11 dc in ring; join with sl st in initial ch 1.
Rnd 2: *ch 5. 2 dtr in next dc. ch 5.** sl st in next dc. Repeat from * 4 times, and from * to ** once more. Join with sl st in sl st.
Rnd 3: sl st in 1st ch of ch 5, and in ch 5 space. ch 1 (counts as dc). 1 dc in same ch 5 space. *[htr, tr] in 1 dtr. ch 1. [tr, htr] in next dtr.** 2 dc in each of the next 2 ch 5 spaces. Repeat from * 4 times, and from * to ** once more. 2 dc in next ch 5 space. Join with sl st in initial ch 1.
Rnd 4: sl st in dc. ch 1 (counts as dc). *dc in htr, and in tr. ch 5, and sl st in 4th ch from hook to form picot. ch 1. Skip ch 1 space. dc in next tr, in htr, and in 1 dc. ch 1.** Skip 2 dc, and dc in 1 dc. Repeat from * 4 times, and from * to ** once more. Join with sl st in initial ch 1. Finish off; weave in ends.

83 TARYN
See page 36 in the showcase

This design is named after a Russian term referring to ground that has been frozen for more than one season.

Finished diameter: 89mm (3½in)
Thread required: 9.1m (10yd)

Foundation ring: ch 6; join with sl st in first ch.
Rnd 1: ch 1 (counts as first dc). 11 dc in ring; join with sl st in initial ch 1.
Rnd 2: ch 5 (counts as dtr). dtr in same stitch as last sl st (the stitch that joined Rnd 1). 2 dtr in dc. *ch 2. 2 dtr in each of the next 2 dc. Repeat from * 4 times. ch 2. Join with sl st in 5th ch of initial ch 5.
Rnd 3: ch 2 (counts as htr). *dc in 2 dtr. htr in 1 dtr. [tr, dtr, ch 2, dtr, tr] in ch 2 point.** htr in 1 dtr. Repeat from * 4 times, and from * to ** once more. Join with sl st in 2nd ch of initial ch 2.
Rnd 4: ch 1 (counts as dc). dc in 1 dc. *ch 7, and sl st in 4th ch from hook to form picot. ch 8, and sl st in 8th ch from hook. ch 4, and sl st in 4th ch from hook. sl st in 3rd and 2nd ch of ch 7. ch 1. dc in next dc. dc in htr, in tr, and in dtr. 2 dc in ch 2 point. ch 4 and sl st in 4th ch from hook. 2 dc in same ch 2 point.** dc in dtr, in tr, in htr, and in 1 dc. Repeat from * 4 times, and from * to ** once more. dc in dtr, and in tr. Join with sl st in initial ch 1. Finish off; weave in ends.

A fall wind is a cold wind whose heavy air accelerates as it moves downhill.

Finished diameter: 86mm (3⅜in)
Thread required: 10.1m (11yd)

Foundation ring: ch 6; join with sl st in first ch.
Rnd 1: ch 1 (counts as first dc). 11 dc in ring; join with sl st in initial ch 1.
Rnd 2: ch 3 (counts as tr). *ch 2. dtr in 1 dc. ch 2.** tr in 1 dc. Repeat from * 4 times, and from * to ** once more. Join with sl st in 3rd ch of initial ch 3.
Rnd 3: sl st in next ch 2 space. ch 1 (counts as dc). htr and tr in same ch 2 space. *[tr, ch 2, tr] in dtr. [tr, htr, dc] in ch 2 space.** [dc, htr, tr] in next ch 2 space. Repeat from * 4 times, and from * to ** once more. Join with sl st in initial ch 1.
Rnd 4: sl st in htr, in 2 tr, and in ch 2 point. ch 1 (counts as dc). ch 8. dc in same ch 2 point. *ch 8. [dc, ch 8, dc] in next ch 2 point. Repeat from * 4 times. ch 8. Join with sl st in initial ch 1.
Rnd 5: sl st in ch 8 loop. ch 1 (counts as dc). In the same ch 8 loop, work the following sequence of stitches: [dc, ch 3, dc, ch 3, dc, ch 6, dc, ch 3, dc, ch 3, 2 dc]. *In the next ch 8 space (between loops), work the following stitches: [2 dc, 2 htr, ch 1, 2 htr, 2 dc].** In the next ch 8 loop, work the following sequence of stitches: [2 dc, ch 3, dc, ch 3, dc, ch 6, dc, ch 3, dc, ch 3, 2 dc]. Repeat from * 4 times, and from * to ** once more. Join with sl st in initial ch 1. Finish off; weave in ends.

85 SNOWSTORM
See page 37 in the showcase

This large, fluffy flake could have floated to the ground at the beginning of a November snowstorm.

Finished diameter: 89mm (3½in)
Thread required: 10.1m (11yd)

Foundation ring: ch 4; join with sl st in first ch.
Rnd 1: ch 3 (counts as tr). *ch 3. tr in ring. Repeat from * 4 times. ch 3, and join in 3rd ch of initial ch 3.
Rnd 2: sl st in ch 3 space. ch 3 (counts as tr). tr in same space. ch 2; 2 tr in same ch 3 space. [2 tr, ch 2, 2 tr] in each of the 5 remaining ch 3 spaces. Join with sl st in 3rd ch of initial ch 3.
Rnd 3: ch 3 (counts as tr). tr in tr. *[tr, ch 2, tr] in ch 2 point.** tr in 4 tr. Repeat from * 4 times, and from * to ** once more. tr in 2 tr. Join in 3rd ch of initial ch 3.
Rnd 4: ch 1 (counts as dc). dc in 2 tr. *[dc, ch 1, tr, ch 1, dc] in ch 2 point. dc in 3 tr. ch 2.** dc in next 3 tr. Repeat from * 4 times, and from * to ** once more. Join with sl st in initial ch 1.
Rnd 5: sl st in 3 dc. ch 1 (counts as dc). ch 4, and dc in same dc as last sl st. *ch 1. dc in next tr (at point). [ch 6, and sl st in 6th ch from hook] 3 times. dc in same tr as last dc. ch 1. [dc, ch 4, dc] in next dc. ch 2. Skip 3 dc, and [dc, ch 3, dc] in next ch 2 space (halfway between points). ch 2.** Skip 3 dc and [dc, ch 4, dc] in 1 dc. Repeat from * 4 times, and from * to ** once more. Join with sl st in initial ch 1. Finish off; weave in ends.

86 MINUANO
See page 36 in the showcase

This heavy, textured snowflake is named after a cold, southwesterly winter wind in southern Brazil.

Finished diameter: 76mm (3in)
Thread required: 9.1m (10yd)

Foundation ring: ch 6; join with sl st in first ch.
Rnd 1: ch 3 (counts as tr). 1 tr in ring. *ch 2. 2 tr in ring. Repeat from * 4 times. ch 2. Join with sl st in 3rd ch of initial ch 3.
Rnd 2: sl st in tr, and in ch 2 space. ch 3 (counts as tr). In same ch 2 space work: tr, ch 2, and 2 tr. [2 tr, ch 2, 2 tr] in each of the 5 remaining ch 2 spaces. Join with sl st in 3rd ch of initial ch 3.
Rnd 3: ch 1 (counts as dc). dc in tr. *[dc, ch 3, dc] in ch 2 point.** dc in 4 tr. Repeat from * 4 times, and from * to ** once more. dc in 2 tr. Join with sl st in initial ch 1.
Rnd 4: ch 1 (counts as dc). *Skip 2 dc; 7 tr in next ch 3 point.** Skip 2 dc, and dc in 2 dc. Repeat from * 4 times, and from * to ** once more. Skip 2 dc, and dc in 1 dc. Join with sl st in initial ch 1.
Rnd 5: sl st in tr. ch 1 (counts as dc). *ch 2. [dc, ch 2] in each of the next 2 tr. [dc, ch 6, dc] in next tr. [ch 2, dc] in each of the next 3 tr. ch 2.** Skip 2 dc, and dc in 1 tr. Repeat from * 4 times, and from * to ** once more. Join with sl st in initial ch 1. Finish off; weave in ends.

GALLEGO
See page 39 in the showcase

This majestic snowflake is named after a cold and sharp north wind in Spain and Portugal.

Finished diameter: 95mm (3¾in)
Thread required: 9.1m (10yd)

Foundation ring: ch 6; join with sl st in first ch.
Rnd 1: ch 1 (counts as dc). 11 dc in ring; join with sl st in initial ch 1.
Rnd 2: ch 1 (counts as dc). *ch 4. Skip 1 dc, and dc in 1 dc. Repeat from * 4 times. ch 4. Join with sl st in initial ch 1.
Rnd 3: sl st in ch 4 space, and ch 1 (counts as dc). tr in same space. ch 2. [tr; dc] in same ch 4 space. [dc, tr, ch 2, tr, dc] in each of the 5 remaining ch 4 spaces. Join with sl st in initial ch 1.
Rnd 4: ch 3 (counts as tr). *ch 3. dc in next ch 2 point. ch 3.** Skip tr, and tr in 2 dc. Repeat from * 4 times, and from * to ** once more. Skip tr, and tr in dc. Join with sl st in 3rd ch of initial ch 3.
Rnd 5: ch 3 (counts as tr). tr in same stitch as last sl st (the stitch that joined Rnd 4). *2 dc in ch 3 space. dc in dc. 2 dc in next ch 3 space. 2 tr in 1 tr. ch 2.** 2 tr in next tr. Repeat from * 4 times, and from * to ** once more. Join with sl st in 3rd ch of initial ch 3.
Rnd 6: ch 1 (counts as dc). dc in tr. *dc in 2 dc. ch 3. Skip 1 dc, and dc in 2 dc. dc in 2 tr. dc in ch 2 space. ch 5, and sl st in 5th ch from hook to form picot. ch 8, and sl st in 4th ch from hook. ch 3, and sl st in 1st ch of ch 8. ch 5, and sl st in 5th ch from hook. dc in same ch 2 space as last dc.** dc in 2 tr. Repeat from * 4 times, and from * to ** once more. Join with sl st in initial ch 1. Finish off; weave in ends.

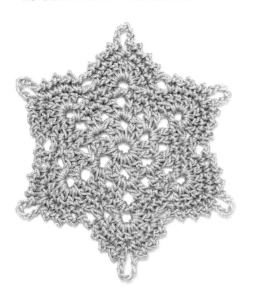

88 AUTAN NOIR
See page 39 in the showcase

The Autan is a strong southeast wind in south-central France. Most of the time, it is associated with clear, dry weather, and called the Autan Blanc ('White Autan'). Occasionally, however, it brings fog, rain or snow, and is called the Autan Noir ('Black Autan').

Finished diameter: 86mm (3⅜in)
Thread required: 10.1m (11yd)

Foundation ring: ch 6; join with sl st in first ch.
Rnd 1: ch 1 (counts as first dc). 11 dc in ring; join with sl st in initial ch 1.
Rnd 2: ch 1 (counts as dc). dc in 1 dc. *ch 5. dc in 2 dc. Repeat from * 4 times. ch 5. Join with sl st in initial ch 1.
Rnd 3: ch 1 (counts as dc). *ch 2. dc in dc. ch 3. tr in top of ch 5 petal. ch 3.** dc in next dc. Repeat from * 4 times, and from * to ** once more. Join with sl st in initial ch 1.
Rnd 4: sl st in ch 2 point. ch 1 (counts as dc). *3 dc in next ch 3 space. [dc, ch 3, dc] in tr. 3 dc in next ch 3 space.** 1 dc in next ch 2 point (halfway between petals). Repeat from * 4 times, and from * to ** once more. Join with sl st in initial ch 1.
Rnd 5: ch 3 (counts as tr). *ch 4. [dc, ch 8, dc] in next ch 3 point. ch 4.** Skip 4 dc, and tr in 1 dc. Repeat from * 4 times, and from * to ** once more. Join with sl st in 3rd ch of initial ch 3.
Rnd 6: ch 1 (counts as dc). *3 dc in ch 4 space. Work the following sequence in the next ch 8 loop: [2 dc, ch 3, dc, ch 4, dc, ch 6, dc, ch 4, dc, ch 3, 2 dc]. 3 dc in next ch 4 space.** dc in tr. Repeat from * 4 times, and from * to ** once more. Join with sl st in initial ch 1. Finish off; weave in ends.

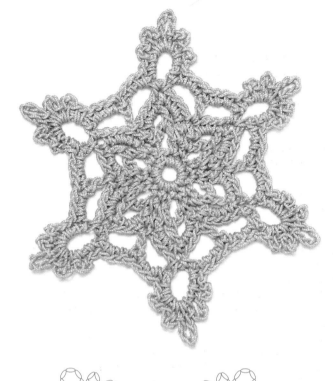

89 SNOWDRIFT
See page 38 in the showcase

This soft-edged snowflake would be at home in a drift of powdery, windblown snow.

Finished diameter: 89mm (3½in)
Thread required: 11m (12yd)

Foundation ring: ch 6; join with sl st in first ch.
Rnd 1: ch 1 (counts as dc). 11 dc in ring; join with sl st in initial ch 1.
Rnd 2: ch 1 (counts as dc). *ch 4. Skip 1 dc, and dc in 1 dc. Repeat from * 4 times. ch 4. Join with sl st in initial ch 1.
Rnd 3: sl st in ch 4 space, and ch 1 (counts as dc). tr in same space. ch 2. [tr; dc] in same ch 4 space. [dc, tr, ch 2, tr, dc] in each of the 5 remaining ch 4 spaces. Join with sl st in initial ch 1.
Rnd 4: sl st in tr, and in ch 2 point. ch 1 (counts as dc). *ch 7. dc in next ch 2 point. Repeat from * 4 times. ch 7. Join with sl st in initial ch 1.
Rnd 5: sl st in ch 7 space, and ch 3 (counts as tr). 4 tr in same space. ch 2, and 5 tr in same ch 7 space. [5 tr, ch 2, 5 tr] in each of the 5 remaining ch 7 spaces. Join with sl st in 3rd ch of initial ch 3.
Rnd 6: ch 3 (counts as tr). 2 tr in same stitch as last sl st (the stitch that joined Rnd 5). *ch 2. 1 dc in next ch 2 point. ch 2. Skip 4 tr. 3 tr in 1 tr. ch 2.** 3 tr in next tr. Repeat from * 4 times, and from * to ** once more. Join with sl st in 3rd ch of initial ch 3.
Rnd 7: sl st in 2 tr, and in ch 2 space. ch 1 (counts as dc). *ch 3. dc in next ch 2 space. ch 4. [dc, ch 8, dc] in ch 2 point. ch 4.** dc in next ch 2 space. Repeat from * 4 times, and from * to ** once more. Join with sl st in initial ch 1. Finish off; weave in ends.

90 WHITE DEW

See page 39 in the showcase

White dew is a name for dew that has been frozen to a glaze by dropping temperatures. After freezing, it might attract a few lacy flakes like this one.

Finished diameter: 83mm (3¼in)
Thread required: 7.3m (8yd)

Foundation ring: ch 6; join with sl st in first ch.
Rnd 1: ch 1 (counts as dc). 11 dc in ring; join with sl st in initial ch 1.
Rnd 2: ch 3 (counts as tr). tr in dc. *ch 3. tr in 2 dc. Repeat from * 4 times. ch 3. Join with sl st in initial ch 1.
Rnd 3: ch 1 (counts as dc). dc in tr. *[dc, tr, ch 4, tr, dc] in next ch 3 point.** dc in 2 tr. Repeat from * 4 times, and from * to ** once more. Join with sl st in initial ch 1.
Rnd 4: sl st in 2 dc. ch 1 (counts as dc). *dc in tr. dc in the next ch 4 point. ch 6, and sl st in 6th ch from hook to form loop. [dc, tr] in same ch 4 point. ch 7, and sl st in 6th ch from hook. [ch 6, and sl st in 6th ch from hook] 2 times. sl st in 1st ch of ch 7. [tr, dc] in the same ch 4 point. ch 6, and sl st in 6th ch from hook. dc in same ch 4 point. dc in tr, and in 1 dc. ch 1.** Skip 2 dc, and dc in 1 dc. Repeat from * 4 times, and from * to ** once more. Join with sl st in initial ch 1. Finish off; weave in ends.

91 CRIVETZ
See page 38 in the showcase

This beautiful pattern is named after the Crivetz, a cold, north-to-east wind in Romania.

Finished diameter: 83mm (3¼in)
Thread required: 9.1m (10yd)

Foundation ring: ch 6; join with sl st in first ch.
Rnd 1: ch 1 (counts as first dc). 11 dc in ring; join with sl st in initial ch 1.
Rnd 2: ch 3 (counts as tr). tr in 1 dc. *ch 5. tr in 2 dc. Repeat from * 4 times. ch 5. Join with sl st in 3rd ch of initial ch 3.
Rnd 3: ch 1 (counts as dc). *ch 2. dc in tr. [dc, htr, tr, ch 4, tr, htr, dc] in ch 5 space.** dc in 1 tr. Repeat from * 4 times, and from * to ** once more. Join with sl st in initial ch 1.
Rnd 4: sl st in ch 2 point. ch 1 (counts as dc). *ch 2. [dc, ch 6, dc, ch 10, dc, ch 6, dc] in next ch 4 point (at the top of the next petal). ch 2.** dc in next ch 2 point (halfway between petals). Repeat from * 4 times, and from * to ** once more. Join with sl st in initial ch 1.
Rnd 5: ch 3 (counts as tr). *4 dc in first ch 6 loop of next cluster. [3 dc, ch 4, 3 dc] in ch 10 loop. 4 dc in last ch 6 loop of cluster.** Skip 1 dc (at the end of the cluster), and tr in next dc (halfway between clusters). Repeat from * 4 times, and from * to ** once more. Join with sl st in 3rd ch of initial ch 3. Finish off; weave in ends.

92 PERMAFROST
See page 38 in the showcase

This complex little snowflake might come to rest in a region of permafrost, or permanently frozen ground.

Finished diameter: 83mm (3¼in)
Thread required: 9.1m (10yd)

Foundation ring: ch 6; join with sl st in first ch.
Rnd 1: ch 1 (counts as first dc). 11 dc in ring; join with sl st in initial ch 1.
Rnd 2: *ch 5. 2 dtr in next dc. ch 5.** sl st in next dc. Repeat from * 4 times, and from * to ** once more. Join with sl st in sl st.
Rnd 3: sl st in 1st ch of ch 5, and in ch 5 space. ch 1(counts as dc). 1 dc in same ch 5 space. *[htr; tr] in 1 dtr. ch 1. [tr; htr] in next dtr.** 2 dc in each of the next 2 ch 5 spaces. Repeat from * 4 times, and from * to ** once more. 2 dc in next ch 5 space. Join with sl st in initial ch 1.
Rnd 4: ch 1 (counts as dc). *ch 5. tr in next ch 1 space (at point). ch 5. Skip tr, htr, and 1 dc.** dc in 2 dc. Repeat from * 4 times, and from * to ** once more. dc in 1 dc. Join with sl st in initial ch 1.
Rnd 5: sl st in ch 5 space. ch 1 (counts as dc). 4 dc in same ch 5 space. *[dc, ch 2, dc] in tr. 5 dc in next ch 5 space. ch 8, and sl st in 4th ch from hook. ch 2. sl st in 2nd and 1st ch of ch 8.** Skip 2 dc; 5 dc in next ch 5 space. Repeat from * 4 times, and from * to ** once more. Join with sl st in initial ch 1. Finish off; weave in ends.

93 ICE FRONT
See page 39 in the showcase

It's easy to picture this angular flake falling past an ice front (the high, cliff-like edge of an ice shelf), and down to the sea.

Finished diameter: 95mm (3¾in)
Thread required: 15.5m (17yd)

Foundation ring: ch 6; join with sl st in first ch.
Rnd 1: ch 3 (counts as first tr). 11 tr in ring; join with sl st in 3rd ch of initial ch 3.
Rnd 2: ch 3 (counts as tr). 2 tr in each of next 11 tr. tr in sl st (the stitch that joined Rnd 1); join with sl st in 3rd ch of initial ch 3.
Rnd 3: *ch 5. dtr in 2 tr. ch 5.** sl st in 2 tr. Repeat from * 4 times, and from * to ** once more. sl st in tr, and join with sl st in sl st.
Rnd 4: *3 dc and 1 htr in next ch 5 space. [tr, dtr] in next dtr. [dtr, tr] in next dtr. 1 htr and 3 dc in next ch 5 space. Skip 1 sl st, and sl st in 1 sl st (at start of next petal). Repeat from * 5 times.
Rnd 5: sl st in 3 dc, in htr, in tr, and in 1 dtr. sl st between the 2 dtr at the top of the petal. ch 1 (counts as dc). *ch 6. Skip dtr; skip tr; skip htr; and skip 3 dc. dtr in sl st (between petals). ch 6.** dc between the 2 dtr at the top of the next petal. Repeat from * 4 times, and from * to ** once more. Join with sl st in initial ch 1.
Rnd 6: sl st in ch 6 space. ch 3 (counts as tr); 5 tr in same space. 6 tr in next ch 6 space. *[tr, ch 3, tr] in dc. 6 tr in each of the next two ch 6 spaces. Repeat from * 4 times. [tr, ch 3, tr] in the sl st that joined Rnd 5. Join with sl st in 3rd ch of initial ch 3.
Rnd 7: ch 1 (counts as dc). dc in 12 tr. *[2 dc, ch 2, 2 dc] in ch 3 point.** dc in 14 tr. Repeat from * 4 times, and from * to ** once more. dc in tr. Join with sl st in initial ch 1. Finish off; weave in ends.

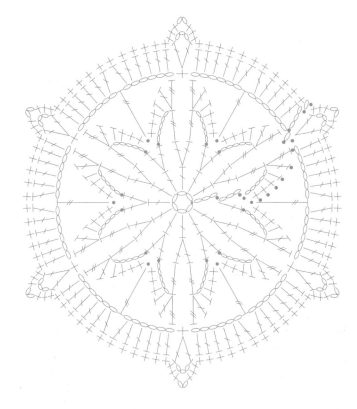

94 | BURIA
See page 38 in the showcase

This elegant crystal could be blown away on the Buria, a Bulgarian term for a cold fall wind.

Finished diameter: 102mm (4in)
Thread required: 11.9m (13yd)

Foundation ring: ch 6; join with sl st in first ch.
Rnd 1: ch 1 (counts as first dc). 11 dc in ring; join with sl st in initial ch 1.
Rnd 2: ch 5 (counts as dtr). *ch 2. dtr in next dc. Repeat from * 10 times. ch 2. Join with sl st in 5th ch of initial ch 5.
Rnd 3: sl st in ch 2 space. ch 3 (counts as tr). 2 tr in same space. 3 tr in next ch 2 space. *ch 2. 3 tr in each of the next 2 ch 2 spaces. Repeat from * 4 times. ch 2. Join with sl st in 3rd ch of initial ch 3.
Rnd 4: ch 1 (counts as dc). dc in 2 tr. *ch 2. dc in 3 tr. [dc, tr] in ch 2 space. ch 6, and sl st in 6th ch from hook to form loop. [tr, dc] in same ch 2 space as last tr.** dc in 3 tr. Repeat from * 4 times, and from * to ** once more. Join with sl st in initial ch 1.
Rnd 5: sl st in 2 dc, and in ch 2 point. ch 1 (counts as dc). *ch 6, and sl st in 6th ch from hook to form loop. dc in same ch 2 space. Skip 3 dc. tr in dc, and in tr. dc in ch 6 loop. ch 6, and sl st in 6th ch from hook. 2 dc in same ch 6 loop as last dc. ch 6, and sl st in 6th ch from hook. ch 8, and sl st in 8th ch from hook. ch 6, and sl st in 6th ch from hook. 2 dc in same loop as last dc. ch 6, and sl st in 6th ch from hook. dc in same loop as last dc. tr in tr, and in dc.** Skip 3 dc, and dc in next ch 2 point. Repeat from * 4 times, and from * to ** once more. Join with sl st in initial ch 1. Finish off; weave in ends.

95 GRAUPEL
See page 40 in the showcase

This sharp-edged snowflake takes its name from a term for icy snow pellets.

Finished diameter: 79mm (3⅛in)
Thread required: 11.9m (13yd)

Foundation ring: ch 6; join with sl st in first ch.
Rnd 1: ch 3 (counts as first tr). 11 tr in ring; join with sl st in 3rd ch of initial ch 3.
Rnd 2: ch 3 (counts as tr). 2 tr in each of next 11 tr. tr in sl st (the stitch that joined Rnd 1); join with sl st in 3rd ch of initial ch 3.
Rnd 3: ch 3 (counts as tr). *ch 3. skip 1 tr, and tr in 1 tr. Repeat from * 10 times. ch 3. Join with sl st in 3rd ch of initial ch 3.
Rnd 4: sl st in next ch 3 space. ch 1 (counts as dc); 3 dc in same space. 4 dc in next ch 3 space. *ch 2. 4 dc in each of the next two ch 3 spaces. Repeat from * 4 times. ch 2. Join with sl st in initial ch 1.
Rnd 5: ch 1 (counts as dc). dc in 3 dc. *ch 2, and dc in 4 dc. [dc, ch 8, dc] in ch 2 space.** dc in 4 dc. Repeat from * 4 times, and from * to ** once more. Join with sl st in initial ch 1.
Rnd 6: sl st in 3 dc, and in ch 2 space. ch 1 (counts as dc). *ch 4. Skip 4 dc; sl st in 1 dc. [3 dc, htr, tr, ch 1, tr, htr, 3 dc] in ch 8 loop. sl st in next dc. ch 4.** Skip 4 dc; dc in next ch 2 space. Repeat from * 4 times, and from * to ** once more. Join with sl st in initial ch 1.
Rnd 7: ch 1 (counts as dc). *ch 4. sl st in next sl st. ch 2. Skip 2 dc; dc in 1 dc. dc in htr and tr. [dc, ch 2, dc] in ch 1 space. dc in tr, in htr, and in dc. ch 2. Skip 2 dc, and sl st in sl st. ch 4.** dc in next dc (halfway between petals). Repeat from * 4 times, and from * to ** once more. Join with sl st in initial ch 1. Finish off; weave in ends.

96 NÉVÉ
See page 41 in the showcase

This large flake could have drifted to Earth on an area of névé, old snow at the head of a glacier.

Finished diameter: 83mm (3¼in)
Thread required: 11m (12yd)

Foundation ring: ch 6; join with sl st in first ch.
Rnd 1: ch 3 (counts as tr), 11 tr in ring; join with sl st in 3rd ch of initial ch 3.
Rnd 2: ch 2 (counts as htr). *ch 2. htr in next tr. Repeat from * 10 times. ch 2; join with sl st in 2nd ch of initial ch 2.
Rnd 3: sl st in next ch 2 space; ch 3 (counts as tr). 2 tr in same space. 3 tr in next ch 2 space. *ch 1. 3 tr in each of the next 2 ch 2 spaces. Repeat from * 4 times. ch 1; join with sl st in 3rd ch of ch 3.
Rnd 4: ch 3 (counts as tr). tr in 1 tr. *dc in 2 tr. tr in 2 tr. [tr, ch 3, tr] in ch 1 space.** tr in 2 tr. Repeat from * 4 times, and from * to ** once more. Join with sl st in 3rd ch of initial ch 3.
Rnd 5: ch 1 (counts as dc). dc in tr, in 2 dc, and in 3 tr. *[dc, ch 8, dc, ch 8, dc, ch 8, dc] in next ch 3 space.** dc in 3 tr, in 2 dc, and in 3 tr. Repeat from * 4 times, and from * to ** once more. dc in tr. Join with sl st in initial ch 1.
Rnd 6: sl st in 7 dc, and in first 2 ch of ch 8 loop. sl st in loop; ch 1 (counts as dc). 3 dc in same loop. [3 dc, ch 2, 3 dc] in next loop (the second loop of this cluster). 4 dc in next loop (the third of this cluster). *ch 3. In next cluster, 4 dc in first loop; [3 dc, ch 2, 3 dc] in second loop; 4 dc in third loop. Repeat from * 4 times. ch 3. Join with sl st in initial ch 1. Finish off; weave in ends.

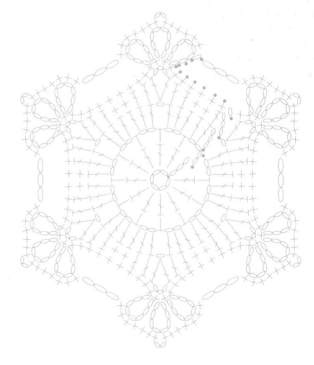

97 FLANDERS STORM
See page 40 in the showcase

This sophisticated star might be found glittering on a branch after a Flanders storm (a heavy snowfall in England).

Finished diameter: 89mm (3½in)
Thread required: 15.5m (17yd)

Foundation ring: ch 6; join with sl st in first ch.
Rnd 1: ch 1 (counts as dc). 11 dc in ring; join with sl st in initial ch 1.
Rnd 2: ch 3 (counts as tr). tr in 1 dc. *ch 3. tr in 2 dc. Repeat from * 4 times. ch 3. Join with sl st in 3rd ch of initial ch 3.
Rnd 3: ch 3 (counts as tr). tr in tr. *2 tr in ch 3 space. ch 8, and sl st in 8th ch from hook to form loop. 2 tr in same ch 3 space.** tr in 2 tr. Repeat from * 4 times, and from * to ** once more. Join with sl st in 3rd ch of initial ch 3.
Rnd 4: ch 1 (counts as dc). *ch 2. dc in 3 tr. dc in ch 8 loop. [ch 6, and dc in same ch 8 loop] 5 times.** dc in 3 tr. Repeat from * 4 times, and from * to ** once more. dc in 2 tr. Join with sl st in initial ch 1.
Rnd 5: sl st in ch 2 point, and ch 1 (counts as dc). *ch 1. 3 dc in each of the next 5 ch 6 loops. ch 1.** dc in next ch 2 point (halfway between loop clusters). Repeat from * 4 times, and from * to ** once more. Join with sl st in initial ch 1.
Rnd 6: ch 1 (counts as dc). *dc in next 7 dc. ch 4. Skip 1 dc (at top of cluster), and dc in 7 dc.** dc in next dc (between clusters). Repeat from * 4 times, and from * to ** once more. Join with sl st in initial ch 1.
Rnd 7: sl st in 4 dc. ch 1 (counts as dc). dc in 3 dc. *[dc, ch 2, dc] in ch 4 point. dc in 4 dc. ch 6.** Skip 7 dc, and dc in next 4 dc. Repeat from * 4 times, and from * to ** once more. Join with sl st in initial ch 1. Finish off; weave in ends.

98 BLUE ICE
See page 40 in the showcase

Blue ice consists of large, single ice crystals, and is usually found in glaciers.

Finished diameter: 95mm (3¾in)
Thread required: 16.5m (18yd)

Foundation ring: ch 6; join with sl st in first ch.
Rnd 1: ch 3 (counts as tr). 11 tr in ring; join with sl st in 3rd ch of initial ch 3.
Rnd 2: ch 1 (counts as dc). *ch 2. dc in next tr. Repeat from * 10 times. ch 2. Join with sl st in initial ch 1.
Rnd 3: sl st in next ch 2 space; ch 1 (counts as dc). dc in same ch 2 space. 2 dc in each of the 11 remaining ch 2 spaces. Join with sl st in initial ch 1.
Rnd 4: *ch 5; dtr in 2 dc. ch5.** sl st in 2 dc. Repeat from * 4 times, and from * to ** once more. sl st in dc, and in sl st.
Rnd 5: *[3 dc, htr] in ch 5 space. [tr, dtr] in 1 dtr. [dtr, tr] in 1 dtr. [htr, 3 dc] in ch 5 space. Skip 1 sl st, and sl st in 1 sl st (at start of next petal). Repeat from * 5 times.
Rnd 6: sl st in 3 dc, in htr, in tr, and in dtr. sl st between the 2 dtr at the top of the petal. ch 1 (counts as dc). *ch 6. Skip dtr, skip tr, skip htr, and skip 3 dc. dtr in the next sl st (between petals). ch 6.** dc between the 2 dtr at top of next petal. Repeat from * 4 times, and from * to ** once. Join with sl st in initial ch 1.
Rnd 7: sl st in next ch 6 space. ch 5 (counts as dtr). [2 tr, 2 htr, 3 dc] in same ch 6 space. *[3 dc, 2 htr, 2 tr, dtr] in next ch 6 space.** 2 dtr in next dc (at point). [dtr, 2 tr, 2 htr, 3 dc] in next ch 6 space. Repeat from * 4 times, and from * to ** once more. 2 dtr in the sl st at the point. Join with sl st in 5th ch of ch 5.
Rnd 8: ch 1 (counts as dc). dc in 2 tr, in 2 htr, and in 2 dc. *ch 1. Skip 2 dc. dc in 2 dc, in 2 htr, in 2 tr, and in 1 dtr. [dc, htr] in 1 dtr. ch 2. [htr, dc] in next dtr.** dc in dtr, in 2 tr, in 2 htr, and in 2 dc. Repeat from * 4 times, and from * to ** once more. Join with sl st in initial ch 1. Finish off; weave in ends.

99 GALE
See page 41 in the showcase

This giant snowflake might be picked up and carried for miles by a winter gale.

Finished diameter: 105mm (4⅛in)
Thread required: 12.8m (14yd)

Foundation ring: ch 6; join with sl st in first ch.
Rnd 1: ch 1 (counts as dc). 11 dc in ring; join with sl st in initial ch 1.
Rnd 2: ch 3 (counts as tr). tr in 1 dc. *ch 3. tr in 2 dc. Repeat from * 4 times. ch 3; join in 3rd ch of initial ch 3.
Rnd 3: sl st in tr, and in ch 3 space. ch 2 (counts as htr). [tr, ch 2, tr, htr] in same ch 3 space. *ch 1. In next ch 3 space, [htr, tr, ch 2, tr, htr]. Repeat from * 4 times. ch 1. Join with sl st in 2nd ch of initial ch 2.
Rnd 4: ch 1 (counts as dc). *tr in tr. [tr, ch1, tr] in ch 2 point. tr in tr. dc in htr. sl st in ch 1 space.** dc in htr. Repeat from * 4 times, and from * to ** once more. Join with sl st in initial ch 1.
Rnd 5: sl st in 2 tr, and in ch 1 point. ch 1 (counts as dc). *ch 5; dtr in next sl st (halfway between points). ch 5.** dc in next ch 1 point. Repeat from * 4 times, and from * to ** once more. Join with sl st in initial ch 1.
Rnd 6: sl st in ch 5 space. ch 5 (counts as dtr). [2 tr, 1 htr, 2 dc] in same ch 5 space. *[2 dc, 1 htr, 2 tr, 1 dtr] in next ch 5 space.** 2 dtr in next dc (at point). [1 dtr, 2 tr, 1 htr, 2 dc] in next ch 5 space. Repeat from * 4 times, and from * to ** once more. 2 dtr in sl st (the stitch that joined Rnd 5). Join with sl st in 5th ch of initial ch 5.
Rnd 7: sl st in 2 tr, in htr, and in 2 dc. ch 1 (counts as dc). ch 6; sl st in ch 1 for loop. *dc in next dc; ch 6. Skip dc, htr, 2 tr, and 1 dtr: dc in 1 dtr. ch 10; sl st in top of the last dc made, for loop. dc in next dtr. ch 6.** Skip dtr, 2 tr, htr, and 1 dc, and dc in 1 dc. ch 6; sl st in top of the last dc made, for loop. Repeat from * 4 times, and from * to ** once more. Join with sl st in ch 1. Finish off; weave in ends.

100 AUSTRU
See page 41 in the showcase

This lacy and intricate design is named after an easterly or southeasterly winter wind in Romania.

Finished diameter: 89mm (3½in)
Thread required: 17.4m (19yd)

Foundation ring: ch 6; join with sl st in first ch.
Rnd 1: ch 1 (counts as first dc). 11 dc in ring; join with sl st in initial ch 1.
Rnd 2: ch 1 (counts as first dc). *[dc, ch 6, dc] in 1 dc.** dc in 1 dc. Repeat from * 4 times, and from * to ** once more. Join with sl st in initial ch 1.
Rnd 3: ch 1 (counts as dc). *[4 dc, ch 2, 4 dc] in next ch 6 loop.** Skip 1 dc (at the bottom of the loop). dc in 1 dc (halfway between loops). Repeat from *4 times, and from * to ** once more. Join with sl st in initial ch 1.
Rnd 4: sl st in 4 dc, and in ch 2 point. ch 1 (counts as dc). *ch 4. skip 4 dc, and tr in 1 dc (halfway between petals). ch 4.** dc in next ch 2 point. Repeat from * 4 times, and from * to ** once more. Join with sl st in initial ch 1.
Rnd 5: sl st in ch 4 space, and ch 3 (counts as first tr). 3 tr in the same ch 4 space *4 tr in next ch 4 space.** [tr, ch 2, tr] in dc. 4 tr in next ch 4 space. Repeat from * 4 times, and from * to ** once more. [tr, ch 2, tr] in sl st (the stitch that joined Rnd 4). Join with sl st in 3rd ch of initial ch 3.
Rnd 6: sl st in next 3 tr. ch 1 (counts as dc); ch 6; dc in next tr. *ch 4. dc in next ch 2 point. [ch 6, and dc in same ch 2 point] 3 times. ch 4.** Skip next 4 tr, and dc in 1 tr. ch 6, dc in next tr. Repeat from * 4 times, and from * to ** once more. Join with sl st in initial ch 1.
Rnd 7: *[3dc, ch 2, 3 dc] in ch 6 loop. sl st in next dc (at the end of the loop). ch 2. dc in ch 4 space. 3 dc in each loop of the next cluster of 3 loops. dc in next ch 4 space. ch 2.** sl st in next dc (at the beginning of the next loop). Repeat from * 4 times, and from * to ** once more. Join with sl st in sl st.
Rnd 8: sl st in 3 dc, and in the ch 2 point at the top of the loop. ch 1 (counts as dc). *ch 4. Skip to the 2nd dc of the next 3 loop cluster (you will skip 3 dc, 1 sl st, the ch 2 space, and 2 dc), and dc in that dc. htr in 1 dc. tr in 1 dc. [dtr, ch 1, dtr] in 1 dc (at the top of the cluster). tr in 1 dc; htr in 1 dc; dc in 1 dc. ch 4.** dc in ch 2 point at the top of the next single loop. Repeat from * 4 times, and from * to ** once more. Join with sl st in initial ch 1. Finish off; weave in ends.

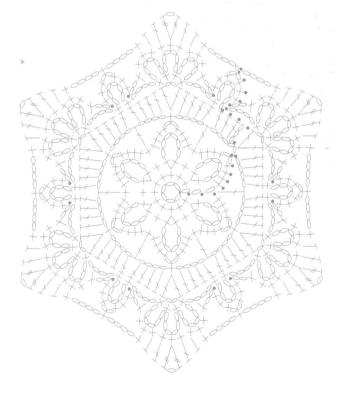

PROJECTS

Snowflakes are so beautiful, so simple and so varied that it can be difficult to stop making them. If you find yourself looking for an excuse to make just a few more, this chapter features some lovely project ideas.

PROJECT 1: TOASTY HAT AND MITTENS

It's one of the childhood joys of an early snowfall: catching a fluffy snowflake on a mittened hand and marvelling over the tiny crystalline patterns as they slowly melt into water droplets. Achieve an equally beautiful but more permanent effect by decorating a cozy fleece hat and mittens with delicate snowflake appliqués.

PROJECT 2: GIFT TAGS AND CARDS

Celebrate the winter holidays or any other special occasion with these pretty handmade gift cards and tags. Using small snowflakes, glue and card stock, you can create fresh, airy designs that are as enjoyable to make as they are to receive.

PROJECT 3: MAGICAL MOBILE

A mobile makes for a mesmerising display as the snowflakes gently spin and float in passing air currents. Crochet snowflakes in a variety of patterns and colors, then use clear thread and short strips of wood to construct your mobile. Finally, hang it from the ceiling, for a captivating addition to a nursery, a sunroom or a child's bedroom.

PROJECT 4: ACCENT PILLOWS

Use appliqué snowflakes to turn a plain throw pillow into a work of art. This project works well with a pillow cover made from heavy, slightly textured fabric (like the linen or chenille ones shown here), and you can combine snowflake designs, crochet threads and fabrics to suit almost any space, whether it's a quiet window seat or a formal living room.

PROJECT 5: HANGING SNOWFLAKES

Hang single snowflakes to decorate windows, doors or the Christmas tree, or make an attractive ornamental display like the one shown that looks great at any time of year. For a bit of sparkle, sew glass seed beads onto your snowflakes in a design of your choice when the snowflakes are complete – the tiny beads won't weigh the snowflakes down, and you can add as many as you wish.

PROJECT 6: FRAMED SNOWFLAKE ART

Frame and hang your snowflakes for attractive, one-of-a-kind pieces of art. Glue a single large snowflake or an arrangement of small ones to a contrasting background, then mount and frame your composition. Since you can design your piece to fit any frame, this is a wonderful way to convert unused frames into gorgeous accent pieces.

PROJECT 7: BLIZZARD SCARF

Wrap yourself in a soft snowflake scarf made from your favourite yarn. (The scarf shown here features the Snow Moon pattern [see page 72] and is crocheted from an alpaca–silk lace-weight yarn.) Make the snowflakes individually and then sew them together, or attach each one to the others as you crochet it, by slip stitching its points to the points of adjoining snowflakes.

INDEX

A

abbreviations 12–13
accent pillows 118–119
Alberta Clipper 29, 66
Alpine Glacier 29, 67
Arctic Mist 24, 51
Aufeis I 28, 68
Aufeis II 29, 69
Austru 41, 109
Autan Noir 39, 98
Auvergnasse 26, 56
Avalanche 30, 77

B

Barber 22, 44
Bise Noir 28, 68
Blizzard 34, 88
blizzard scarf 124–125
blocking 19
blocking board components 11
Blue Ice 40, 107
Bora 27, 62
Boreas 22, 48
Boulbie 35, 88
Burga 31, 76
Buria 38, 103

C

Candle Ice 32, 84
Carcenet 30, 76
cards 114–115
Cavaburd 27, 61
Cierzo 34, 86
Cirque Glacier 33, 79
Crivetz 38, 100
crochet hooks 10, 14
crochet refresher course 14–18
    double crochet 16

double treble 17
foundation chain 15
half treble 16
holding hook and yarn 14
slip knots 14
slip stitch 15
treble 17
working in rounds 18
crochet thread 10, 14
Crystalline Frost 37, 94

D

double crochet 16
double treble 17
Droxtal 23, 47

E

Elvegust 32, 81
equipment 10–11

F

fabric stiffener 11
Fall Wind 37, 95
Firn 24, 55
Firnspiegel 26, 57
Flanders Storm 40, 106
Flurry 23, 47
foundation chain 15
foundation ring 18
framed snowflake art 122–123
Frazil 22, 49
Frost 22, 44
Frost Mist 27, 60

G

Gale 41, 108
Gallego 39, 97
gift tags and cards 114–115

Graupel 40, 104
Guxen 37, 92

H

half treble 16
Halo 27, 62
hanging snowflakes 120–121
hat
    toasty hat and mittens 112–113

I

Ice Crystal I 26, 58
Ice Crystal II 26, 59
Ice Feathers 36, 93
Ice Flower 25, 52
Ice Front 39, 102
Ice Prism 27, 56
Icicle 30, 75

J

Juran 31, 74

K

Kaavie 25, 55
Kaikias 28, 64
Kossava 25, 52

L

Lake Effect 23, 49

M

materials 10–11
Minuano 36, 96
Mistral 32, 78
mittens
    toasty hat and mittens 112–113
mobile, magical 116–117

N

N'Aschi 32, 83
Narbonnais 23, 48
Nemere 31, 72
Nevada 22, 46
Névé 41, 105
Nieve Penitente 28, 63
Nor'Easter I 25, 53
Nor'Easter II 25, 53
Nor'Easter III 24, 54
Nor'Easter IV 25, 54
Norte 26, 58
Norther 27, 61
Northern Lights I 35, 90
Northern Lights II 35, 91
Northern Nanny 31, 78

P

patterns 12–13
    creating your own pattern 13
Permafrost 38, 101
pillows
    accent pillows 118–119
pins 11
Plane Dendrite 33, 84
Polar Glacier 23, 46
Polaris 34, 89
projects
    accent pillows 118–119
    blizzard scarf 124–125
    framed snowflake art 122–123
    gift tags and cards 114–115
    hanging snowflakes 120–121
    magical mobile 116–117
    toasty hat and mittens 112–113

R

Rimed Crystal 31, 73
rounds
    finishing final round 18
    foundation ring 18
    working into ring 18

S

Sansar 35, 87
scarf
    blizzard scarf 124–125
Scharnitzer 30, 74
scissors 10
Sea Ice I 32, 82
Sea Ice II 33, 82
Sea Smoke 36, 92
Sikussak 24, 50
Silver Frost 29, 65
Sleet I 29, 70
Sleet II 30, 70
slip knots 14
slip stitch 15
Snow Mist 24, 50
Snow Moon 31, 72
Snowdrift 38, 99
Snowstorm 37, 96
Spring Snow 23, 45
Squall 26, 60
starch 11
Stellar Crystal 22, 45
stiffening 19
Suestada 33, 80
symbols 12

T

Taku 28, 66
Taryn 36, 94
Thundersnow 28, 64

toasty hat and mittens 112–113
tools 10–11
treble 17
Tundra 35, 86

V

Viuga 30, 71

W

White Buran 24, 51
White Dew 39, 100
Whiteout 34, 85
Winter Solstice 33, 80

ACKNOWLEDGEMENTS

All images are the copyright of Quarto Publishing plc. While every effort has been made to credit contributors, Quarto would like to apologise should there have been any omissions or errors – and would be pleased to make the appropriate correction for future editions of the book.

AUTHOR'S ACKNOWLEDGEMENTS

Thank you to everyone at Quarto for their help and encouragement, and to my family for their support and patience.

Description of rimed crystals is from Kenneth G. Libbrecht's site, SnowCrystals.com: www.its.caltech.edu/~atomic/snowcrystals/.

Definitions of Thundersnow, Snow Moon, and Polaris are from Wikipedia: www.wikipedia.org.

All other meteorological terms and definitions are from the American Meteorological Society's Glossary of Meteorology online: amsglossary.allenpress.com/glossary.